# *Where the Spirit Breathes*

# José I. González Faus

# *Where the Spirit Breathes*

## *Prophetic Dissent in the Church*

Translated by Robert R. Barr

ORBIS BOOKS

**Maryknoll, New York 10545**

Originally published as *La libertad de palabra en la Iglesia y en la teología: Antología comentada*, copyright © 1985 by Editorial Sal Terrae, Apartado 77/39080, Santander, Spain

English translation copyright © 1989 by Orbis Books
Published in the United States by Orbis Books, Maryknoll, NY 10545
Manufactured in the United States of America

**Library of Congress Cataloging-in-Publication Data**

González Faus, José Ignacio.
    [Libertad de palabra en la Iglesia y en la teologia. English]
    Where the Spirit breathes : prophetic dissent in the church / José
I. González Faus : translated by Robert R. Barr.
        p.   cm.
    Translation of: Libertad de palabra en la Iglesia y en la
teologia.
    ISBN 0-88344-363-5
    1. Freedom of speech in the church.   2. Catholic Church—
Doctrines.   I. Title.
BX1746.G56513   1989
262'.8—dc19

                                                                88-36925
                                                                CIP

To God's Holy Church,
that we may love it
as Gustavo Gutiérrez loves it:
"With the love I had before the war"
[Congress of Theology of Madrid, 1984]

# CONTENTS

# FOREWORD

This book is one of those careful, spirited works that may forever revolutionize the way Catholics think about criticism and dissent within the church. González Faus achieves his effect by presenting an anthology of key texts, followed by a thoughtful theological reflection; he succeeds in bringing into focus a dimension of the Catholic tradition which often has been overlooked—or strategically forgotten.

The author puts before us pointed and often surprising examples of Catholic criticism of church authorities, written in the near and distant past. Who could have realized that so many great Catholic saints and scholars were so brutally frank and bold in their critique of church abuses? Here we can peruse texts by well-known thinkers like Augustine, Ignatius, and Karl Rahner, along with those by less famous scholars and observers from a wide range of historical periods. After presenting his selection of sharp accusations and observations, González Faus proceeds to an elucidation of the theological foundations undergirding and justifying this Christian tradition of criticism and fraternal correction.

In reflecting upon this tradition González Faus articulates the best intuitions of Christians with certain unforgettable phrases and statements of his own. When he holds up the Christian ideal of authority and mutual criticism he says, "The church is 'the world inside out'—though it not be such in the eyes of that world." In the Christian community that is "the world inside out," there must be love, liberty, and humility instead of the world's standard operating procedures of pride, domination, and fearfulness. As the author says, "To be authority in the church means to be much more *obliged* to love more."

If one is true to the example of Jesus and to the gospel tradition, then authority will be oriented to loving service, not to aping the wealth and power of the princes of this world. As

González Faus sums up the core of the message of the Christian tradition of dissent, he states that authority must be "desacralized" and "transposed to service," despite the resistance of human sinfulness and inertia. The holiness of the church is demonstrated by the willingness to be corrected from within, because internal criticism, "far from detracting from the sanctity of the church, actually engages it, sets it in operation. . . ." A key and central text in the authentic tradition presented here comes from Augustine:

> With all the devotion of a benign humility, Peter accepted the expression of Paul's productive liberty of love. Peter, then, has given an example for all time to come: all ought to allow themselves to be corrected, even by those who are expected to follow them, if perchance the guides should depart from the right path.

Augustine goes on to say that while Christians must always observe charity, they must also have the courage to give and receive correction for the sake of the gospel. Perhaps we could say that upon this rock — Peter's acceptance of Paul's correction — the church of Jesus Christ has been built.

In his reflections and commentaries González Faus also emphasizes that an abiding Christian concern over the centuries has been to save the church from its temptation to fall into worldly corruptions. The shepherds fail the flock by garnering wealth at the expense of the poor. Or church leaders abuse their power and authority for their own selfish ends. Unfortunately, even when gross personal corruption is absent, authorities can be arrogant, or tempted to cling to security, putting the survival of the church as a worldly institution before fidelity to the gospel message. Scandals and sin will come, but they can never be tamely accepted or ignored by those who truly love the church.

Another of the principles the author highlights within the tradition of dissent is that critics acting out of zealous love must exercise Christian humility as they offer their criticism. If they truly love the church they will struggle against abuses despite the personal price that must be paid. And what suffering and humiliation some of the prophetic critics described here have had to undergo! Critics may be canonized long after their demise, but during their lifetime the most humble, sincere, and holy persons have faced humiliating persecutions. Nevertheless, they persevered and were true to the reforming work of the Holy Spirit.

Love and fidelity inspired Christians to follow Paul's example of courageously confronting the great (inside and outside the church) in defense of the truth of the gospel. Christian critics true to their tradition were—and in the future should be—loving, just, honest, and open; they did not resort cowardly to rumor and whispering. Like critics of the past, critics of the present and future should use common sense. The Catholic tradition counsels critics against the temptation to separate from or sever ties with the church in the mistaken idea that they can ever establish a purified group, free of the failings of other more ordinary sinners. Love demands confrontation and struggle, but also fidelity and loyalty to the ongoing community.

González Faus gives us a wonderful gift when he reveals the fullness and hardiness of the Christian tradition of mutual correction. This understanding will serve us well, now and in the future. We must struggle to reform ourselves as a community as we work to reform the world. Fortunately, the Holy Spirit blows where it listeth and strengthens the minds and hearts of the faithful, raising up prophets and scholarly critics. If this book could be thoroughly assimilated by all Catholics, in and out of authority, we would be well-armed against blandness, tepidity, cowardice, and abuses of authority. Happily, this work is an exemplary model of the once and future tradition González Faus champions: it is humble, charitable, courageous, and infused with Christian hope.

*Sidney Callahan*

# PREFACE

This is a curious book. I speak in it less than anyone else. It is a collection of arguments from authority and behavior. On a first level, this behavior will demonstrate that Christian freedom has been a fact, despite the many afflictions it has had to undergo, and a fact that can no longer be buried, now that we feel the fresh winds of renewal and self-appraisal. But on a deeper level, it will also enable us to surmise the justice of Gregorio Marañón's words: "The merit of truth is almost never that of the one who speaks it. It is nearly always that of the one who knows how to hear it." Both lessons are of the type that convey not an a priori theory, but the very life of the church, which itself becomes a valid tradition when relived and rethought by believers.

Perhaps I ought to say a few words in justification of this anthology. To begin, I wish to make it clear that I realize that the following texts may make for disturbing reading. I feel the same sense of irritation and regard myself as "one body" with those who are disturbed by the texts, for these texts are not my own words. Yet I think of the discomfort as being something like a stomach-ache caused by aspirin that was needed for a headache, or like a headache caused by an analgesic that simply had to be used because of intense pain. To minimize the discomfort, I have taken care to measure out the medicine in small doses. (I could have presented many more texts in Part 1, which includes only forty-one fragments from twenty centuries of history.) And all criticism "from the outside" has been deliberately excluded—not because I think that we should shut ourselves off from such voices, but because I think they should not be utilized in the present argumentation. And so the writers permitted to speak are nearly always saints, ecclesiastics, or other writers of unquestionable loyalty to the church. Thus the selection of texts is clearly limited. It is also, to a large extent, arbitrary. I am not an expert on the whole of church history; nor do I aspire to an Olympic medal for erudition. Perhaps instead of being regarded as a full-fledged anthology, this book should be regarded simply as a collection of examples. And the reader is asked not to forget even for a moment that there is more to the book than Part 1 and its forty-one texts. Part 1 leads into Parts 2, 3, and 4.

Another point I wish to make about this book is that one purpose for my writing it derives from my pastoral experience. Perhaps in our grandparents' time it would have been inappropriate for people who had never had any critical thoughts about the church to know that the saints had not only had those thoughts, but had actually expressed them. Today, however, it will surely be appropriate for persons who so frequently have such thoughts, and feel guilty for having them, to know that the saints, too, have had them, and openly expressed them. Why? Because this experience, assimilated in a spirit of serenity, can transform what many regard as an argument *against* the faith today into an argument *for* the faith. Not a few of the faithful of our days are convinced that God continues to call the church to a serious reform, and that the highest authorities in the church would be doing the church a disservice were they to insist on the unsuitability of such a reform on the grounds that, since the church is holy, it is therefore beyond all reproach. At the same time, I wish to echo the animadversion of these same authorities: a demand for this reform must come not by way of systematic disobedience, manipulation, hostility, or "ecclesial terrorism," but in the sole strength of the Word, and of the element of truth contained in each word of that Word. After all, the truth we seek to express in our human words is ultimately beyond all utterance.

Finally, I pray that both groups may heed the courageous, insightful words that Pope Leo XIII addressed to the clergy of France on September 8, 1899:

> Church historians will the better manifest the divine provenance [of the church], an origin superior to any concept of purely earthly and natural order, the more loyally they will have refused to dissemble the trials and sufferings occasioned this Spouse of Christ by her children's trans-

gressions down through the centuries, be those children her very ministers.

Along more practical lines, two remarks remain to be made. First, besides being incomplete and arbitrary, my selection of texts comes to an abrupt end with the Second Vatican Council. This is intentional. It is not yet possible to gather up and appraise the luxuriance of material that has sprung up in the church since the council, and placidly separate the wheat from the chaff. (There have been both.)

Second, the rationale for the order of the texts is sometimes chronological and sometimes thematic, without distinction. This should not occasion any practical difficulty, although of course the texts could have been presented differently. The crucial element in this book will be the reader's own contribution: reading and meditating on the texts themselves, not my presentation of those texts.

# *Where the Spirit Breathes*

# PART I

# THE FACTS

### The Gospel Will Not Leave the Church in Peace

*Every true and lasting reform has ultimately sprung from the sanctity of men and women who were driven by the love of God and of others. Generous, ready to stand to attention to any call from God, yet confident in themselves because confident in their vocation, they grew to the size of beacons and reformers. On the other hand, any reformatory zeal, which instead of springing from personal purity, flashes out of passion, has produced unrest instead of light, destruction instead of construction, and more than once set up evils worse than those it was out to remedy [Pius XI,* Mit Brennender Sorge, *in* The Papal Documents 1903–39, *ed. Claudia Carlen (Wilmington, N.C.: McGrath, 1981)].*

PUBLIC OPINION IS PART OF THE LEGACY OF ANY NORMAL SOCIETY CONSTITUTED OF HUMAN BEINGS. . . . WHERE NO MANIFESTATION OF PUBLIC OPINION APPEARED, WHERE IT WERE ACTUALLY NECESSARY TO ESTABLISH WHETHER SUCH OPINION EXISTS, WE SHOULD HAVE TO ACCUSE THAT SOCIETY OF A FAILURE, A WEAKNESS, A SOCIAL INFIRMITY. . . .

WE WISH TO ADD A WORD ABOUT PUBLIC OPINION IN THE CHURCH, IN THOSE MATTERS THAT ARE OPEN TO FREE DISCUSSION. THE EXPRESSION OF SUCH OPINION COMES AS A SURPRISE ONLY TO THOSE WHO DO NOT KNOW THE CATHOLIC CHURCH, OR WHO HAVE A FALSE OPINION OF IT. FOR THE CHURCH, TOO, IS A LIVING ORGANISM, AND AN IMPORTANT ELEMENT WOULD BE MISSING FROM ITS LIFE WERE IT TO BE WITHOUT THE EXPRESSION OF PUBLIC OPINION. THE BLAME FOR THIS SHORTCOMING WOULD LIE WITH ITS SHEPHERDS AND FAITHFUL [Pius XII, *Osservatore Romano,* Feb. 18, 1950].

# TEXTS WITH COMMENTARY

*There are those today who would seem to wish to nullify the words of Pius XII cited on the facing page. Some reject the very fact of criticism of the church, rather than the disloyalty to the church or the lack of charity that might be betrayed in a particular criticism. Any criticism of the church, it is argued, is a breach of unity, and therefore can proceed only from a lack of love for the church. It would be difficult to deny a suggestion of this tone in the pope's 1982 visit to Spain, for example.[1]*

*Or it is insisted that the church is our mother, and one never criticizes a mother. Now, while the first part of this assertion is a great truth, the second may imply the unwarranted identification of the body of the church with one or more of its members who may be the object of criticism.*

*The most serious danger of these various attempts to nullify criticism in the church may well be this—if no criticism of the church were ever permitted to exist, then criticism of the church could never be transformed into a criticism, a challenge, and a call for conversion of the very person making the criticism. At all events, the fathers of the church, alluding to Galatians 4:26 ("Jerusalem is our mother"), certainly thought that the prophets' criticism of Jerusalem was validly accommodated to a criticism of the church.*

*Any attempt to discount the words of Pius XII, then, seems futile. When we consider the wide variety of episcopal reaction to the agonizing situations prevailing in Latin America, we cannot escape the thought that, if some of the bishops of that continent incarnate the attitude and behavior of the Good Shepherd, the conduct of others can only be likened to that of the hireling of the Gospel. (I make this appraisal with respect to conduct alone. I make no attempt to pass judgment on subjective intentions.) When we study those situations and view attempts by some forces to repress criticism, we seem to*

*3*

*see a verification of Pius XII's clear, straightforward assertion in the foregoing text. The repression of public opinion never proceeds from the strength of the repressing authority. It proceeds from the internal weakness of that authority. A long series of facts and events in the life of the church — today a part of the tradition of that church — support the conclusion drawn by Pius XII, and compel us to accept the following generalization: curiously, the more the church has been truly alive in souls and peoples, the more lively has been their criticism of the church.*

*This is the datum on which I should now like to concentrate. Let me make a selection from this great series of testimonials. Let me begin with certain passages from a great saint regarded by many today as rather a "conservative" theologian: Saint Bernard of Clairveaux, whose grating tones in the following passages will make nearly all of today's "dissonant" voices sound like sweet harmony. Let us examine a sermon of his to the people on the subject of the bishops, together with a composition dealing with the Roman Curia.*

[1]   Yesterday we were saying that we should like to have leaders who actually guide us along our path, rather than the sort we have now. Our current "leaders" are just the opposite. Not all of those in the Bride's entourage today, not all of her mentors, are friends of the Groom! On the contrary, rare are the ones who are not devoted exclusively to their own interests. They love their perquisites, and they love them more than they love Christ. For they have given themselves over to Mammon. See how elegantly they go forth, arrayed in the splendor of a bride coming forth from her chamber. Would you not take them rather for the Bride, than for the guardians of the Bride? And what, do you imagine, is the source of all this exuberance, this splendor of vesture, this luxury of the festive board, this mass of objects of gold and silver? Why, to be sure, the Bride's dowry! This is why she [the church] is so disfigured today — in disarray, pale, insipid, of such lamentable mien. Do they adorn the Bride? They despoil her. Take care of her? They destroy her. Defend her? They throw her to the wolves. Train her in what is good? They prostitute her. They do not feed their flock, they sacrifice it, they

gobble it up! . . . The prophet says: "They shall devour the sins of my people" — as if to say: they demand money for absolving sins, without in any way concerning themselves with emending the sinners. Show me a bishop not more concerned with discharging his people's purses of their money than their souls of their sins! . . .

Of course it is a waste of time to go on like this. They will pay no attention. I could even write them a letter about all this, and they would not so much as bother to read it. Or if they did chance to peruse it, they would be annoyed with me, instead of with themselves as they ought. . . .

They have inherited the ministry of the apostles, but not their zeal. All wish to be the apostles' successors, but few their imitators. Would that they were as ready to perform their offices as they have been to obtain them! How well the Psalm (37:2) says of them: "My friends and neighbors have struck an alliance against me. . . ."

At the present moment, the Spouse does not find whom she seeks; she is found instead by some whom she seeks not. . . . [Saint Bernard, *Homilia 77 in Canticum Canticorum* (*PL* 183: 1155–56)].

*In the* De Consideratione, *a work of his old age, composed between 1149 and 1152, Saint Bernard writes the following to Pope Eugene III.*

[2] How ever shall I utter what I feel? I know what I shall be told. I shall be told, "How dare you address the pope in this way!" (What other defense can be mounted? Certainly no one can claim that my words are false!) But no, this *is* the way to speak to the pope. How do I know? Because I know what has been done in the past. This manner of discourse may have fallen into *dis*use, but it is not for all that an *ab*use. . . . The only real difficulty with it is that it is displeasing to those who are more the friends of majesty than of verity! Before you came, there were shepherds who devoted their lives to their flock, who gloried in the mission and name of shepherd, who regarded nothing as detrimental to their dignity but what were unwholesome for their flock, who did not seek their own interests, but placed

these, their solicitude, their fortunes, and themselves, at the service of their flock. . . .

And as if they were saying: "I have not come to be served, but to serve," they preached the gospel at no cost to any but themselves. The only profit they extracted from their subjects, their sole pomp and pleasure, was the satisfaction of knowing they were molding a people of God that would please the Lord. . . .

And what has become of all this? It has been replaced by conduct entirely different—other usages altogether. And how much worse they are! The old concern, the anguish, the solicitude, the emulation—this is all still there, you see. But their object has been replaced! For, I assure you—your poverty is not like that of your predecessors. And be further assured, when the locus of power is shifted, relationships change as well. How few there are in our day who look to what the legislator pronounces rather than to what he will bestow! And they know what they are about, for he will bestow—papal privileges! Can you show me a single individual in all your teeming city who has received you as pope without self-interest? The greedier they are for power, the more generous they are in offering you their services! And I should not like to be in the porter's shoes the day they throng to the door and that door does not swing wide at the first knock!

Do I know your people or do I not? Ill-regarded in heaven and on earth, they have gotten their hands on both: the ungodly on God, the impudent on the sacred, the treacherous on one another, the jealous and competitive on their neighbors, the inhumane on strangers. They are unloved because they love not. If they claim to be feared by everyone, it is because they fear everyone. Unwilling to obey, neither do they know how to command. Faithless to their superiors, they tyrannize over their subjects. Unbridled in their own demands, never do they grant the request of another. They make those demands in season and out, wring their hands until they are granted—and then show no gratitude. . . . Yes, I have written at great length. But now you know a great deal about those who press about you!

But back to my original subject. How comes it that all one need do in order to be enriched with the plunder of the churches is to flatter you? "Euge, euge," they cry![2] The life of the poor paves the courts of the wealthy. Silver gleams in the mire, and the race is on—to be won, not by the poor, but by the mighty. I know, you did not originate these doings (or rather, these dyings).[3] But you could halt them. Instead, you, the shepherd, prance about in gold of Ophir like a bride bedecked for her wedding.[4] What good is this to the flock? If I dare say it: this is more a pasture for demons than for the flock. Did Saint Peter do such things? Did Saint Paul amuse himself in this way? You see how the men of the church exercise all their zeal to defend their dignity. For honors, everything; for holiness, next to nothing! Could you not begin to behave with a bit more simplicity and social awareness? There are abundant reasons for you to do so. But then I hear what they tell me at once: "Oh, goodness no! The time is not ripe! It would be inconsistent with his exalted position! After all, one must consider the dignity of the person!" How curious. Everything under the sun must be taken into consideration. Except the will of God. These people have no fear even for their own salvation. Unless perchance they imagine that pomp is salvation and glory is justice!

. . . Of the one whose chair you occupy, Saint Peter, it is not recounted that he strutted about clad in silks, dripping with jewels, plastered with gold, on a white horse, surrounded by soldiers, and followed by a cheering retinue! Somehow, without any of this, Peter still thought he could well enough fulfill the Lord's injunction: "If you love me, feed my sheep!" But have you followed Peter? No, you have followed Constantine.

. . . Promote not those who desire promotion, but those who refuse it. Honor not those who pursue honors, but those who accept them only with reluctance. Elevate those who fear God alone, and who expect nothing from anyone but God; who dauntlessly defend the afflicted and render justice to the lowly of the earth . . . ; who pursue Christ, not gold; who to the kings of the earth are like the Baptist, to the Egyptians like Moses, and to the buyers and sellers in the temple, like Christ; who teach the people rather than condemning them; who do not coddle the rich but frighten them; who do not make the life of the poor still harder, but who offer them reason to hope; who neither prey on them to enslave them nor strut about like their masters; who do not squeeze purses, but renew hearts . . . ; who are lovable not for the profusion of their words but for their conduct; who inspire reverence not by their pomp but by their actions; who are lowly with the lowly and innocent with the innocent, but who answer the harsh with severity . . . ; and who are not in a rush to enrich themselves or their relatives with the widow's dowry and the legacy of the Crucified, but who give freely what they have freely received, and freely do justice to the victims of injustice. . . .

In conclusion: elevate those who keep foremost in mind that the holy Roman Church belongs to God, though it be presided over by you; that it is the mother of the churches, not their mistress; that you are not the bishops' lord, but one of their number, brother to all lovers of God and companion to those who fear him. . . . Be pastor of the nations, teacher of the illiterate, eye of the blind, voice of the dumb, staff of the aged, . . . hammer of tyrants, . . . salt of the earth, light of the world, the Lord's anointed, and very "God" for the pharaohs of this world! [Saint Bernard, *De Consideratione,* book 4, chaps. 2–3 (*PL* 182:773–76)].[5]

*In a treatise entitled* The Customs and Duties of Bishops, *Bernard tells not only the pope but the other bishops how they ought to conduct themselves. Here are some examples of the freedom with which he addresses the latter:*

[3]    They wax indignant with me, and bid me hold my tongue, denying that a monk has the right to judge bishops. Then would they close my eyes, as well, that I might not see what they forbid me to impugn? . . . And were I to fall silent, yet would a voice resound in the church: "Let them not wear sumptuous garments" (1 Tim. 2:9). And these words are addressed to women! Let a bishop blush to hear them spoken to himself! . . . And the hungry and naked will cry out against them: "This is ours that you waste! Your vanities rob us of our necessities" [Saint Bernard, *De Moribus et Officio Episcoporum,* chap. 2 (*PL* 182:815)].

*After the bishops, the clergy must stand in the docket. In the year 1140 Saint Bernard was invited by the bishop of Paris to*

*preach to the students of that great city. The content of his
sermons is collected in a work called* On the Conversion of
the Clergy, *and is intended as a kind of spiritual directory,
although some of its paragraphs will sound like foreshadow-
ings of the finest anticlericalism of later centuries.*

[4]   Woe to you who have stolen not only the key of knowledge,
but that of authority, as well! Ill-content to refuse to enter the
Kingdom yourselves, in a thousand ways you prevent the entry
of those whom you should be helping to come in. You have not
received the keys, you have made off with them! Whence this
all-consuming desire for prelatures, this unbridled ambition, this
frantic insanity for perquisites and sinecures? Who among you
has dared disdain the authority of even the least of the princes
of this world? Who has not rather used that authority to grasp
at ministerial functions or benefices, or indeed simply some crass
commercial advantage? Do not imagine that God approves what
is perpetrated in his great house and broad dominions by all
these vessels of wrath, doomed to destruction. . . .

Our heavenly Father calls "pure of heart" not those who seek
their own interests, but those intent on the concerns of Jesus
Christ—who strive not for what will be most useful to themselves, but what will most redound to the good of the multitude. . . .

We do not wonder, brothers—we who deplore the present
state of the church—we do not wonder that a serpent gives birth
to a scorpion. We do not wonder that they plunder the vineyard
of the Lord who transgress the law of the Lord [Saint Bernard,
*De Conversione ad Clericos,* chap. 19 (*PL* 852–53)].

*No less than bishops and the clergy, monks must feel the sting
of Saint Bernard's prophetic words. Around 1125, at the urg-
ing of William, Abbot of Saint-Thierry, the saint composed a
response to the attacks of the old monks of Cluny, who had
fallen into laxity and so were irritated with Bernard's criticism.*

[5]   One must never criticize what one may be guilty of oneself,
we say. After all, human flesh is weak. Yet will I speak, though
I be charged with audacity for it. I must speak the truth! How
has the light of the world become darkness? How has the salt

of the earth lost its savor? Those who ought to have been the guides and beacons of our life, who ought to have been offering us examples to live by, provide us instead with an example of pridefulness in their works, and of the blind leading the blind. After all—to omit so much else—what spectacle of humility do they present when they parade down the avenue in their great processions, surrounded with their cavalcades and their wide-wigged lackeys? Who comes? Two bishops? No, just one abbot. I should be lying in my teeth were I to deny once seeing an abbot who had in his retinue more than sixty men on horseback. You would think that the ones parading past were not the abbots of monasteries, but barons and princes! Not shepherds of souls, but lords of provinces! Besides all this, they cause to be borne in procession altar cloths, table service, candelabra, great trunks stuffed not with necessary clothing, but with quilts, pillows, and other luxurious adornments for their beds! They are going no more than four leagues from their monastery, and they send ahead their whole bedroom, all their furniture! You would think they were off to war, or going on a safari! [Saint Bernard, *Apologia ad Guillelmum,* chap. 11 *(PL* 182:913–14)].

> *The first few lines of the passage just cited are intended to show why abbots and other religious superiors dare not reform their monks: because of their own laxity. But it also shows us that Bernard did not criticize out of a sense of superiority, or because he claimed to be without the faults he criticizes. The critic knows he is a sinner. His criticism does not spring from a claim to sanctity. But even were the critic to keep silent, the gospel of Jesus would keep on crying out and needling the church.*
>
> *Finally, we should note that in his attack on what he regarded as excessive and luxurious in the church, even in certain famous monasteries, Bernard frequently employed free and vexing language. Perhaps he exaggerated at times. But this does not detract from the core of truth in the principle formulated by the saint as follows: "The walls of the church gleam, while its poor are in need. It plates its stones with gold, while its children go naked" [ibid., chap. 12].*
>
> *These are all the words of a saint. They do not proceed*

*from lovelessness. Far from it. Precisely in the work cited earlier, the* De Consideratione, *Bernard is addressing a pope who had been his pupil and spiritual child. Hence the emphasis on the affection with which he upbraids the Holy Father, for it is this love in his heart that gives him the freedom to speak in this way. He says: "Though you rode on the wings of the wind, you could not deprive me of my affection; for love recognizes a child, even under the tiara."*

*It may also be worthwhile to recall that, great as was his prestige in Europe, Saint Bernard had of course not yet been canonized when he penned these lines! No, he was raised to official sainthood only after having written them. At the time they pricked like needles, and were received with anything but good grace. Their author was actually denounced to the college of cardinals, and he received a cold, harsh letter from Cardinal Emerico about "monks who emerge from their cloisters to harass the Holy See and the Cardinals." Whereupon Saint Bernard lamented: "It seems that when I wage war on outrages, I incur the wrath of the outrageous!"*

*Finally, the reader might remark that many of Saint Bernard's criticisms would be without foundation in the church today. This, thank God, is indeed a fact. Many of them would be. But many others would not. And at all events the question remains: Had there been no critical voices long ago, such as Saint Bernard's, or if such voices had been silenced then — would it be possible today to raise objections that* are *appropriate? Henri Daniel-Rops, one of the most loyal of church historians, writes: "Two circumstances in particular aided the reform. First, the extraordinary latitude permitted, even within the church itself, to criticism or, to use a political expression, to 'self-criticism.' . . . In 1248, Canon Thomas of Chantimpré could calmly relate, in his curious allegorical work,* The Bees, *that, as a certain preacher had been preparing to utter the exordium of his sermon to the Council, he had seen the devil appear, and that the demon had called out to him: 'Don't you know what to say? Just say: "The Princes of Hell salute the Princes of the Church!"' And the good canon was neither arrested nor condemned! . . . "[6]*

*Daniel-Rops then continues: "The second favorable cir-*

*cumstance was that the hierarchy had the moral fiber to ac-
knowledge that such criticisms were justified, and to act
accordingly. Those in authority were not overwhelmed by the
all-too-human reflex to stop the mouths of those whose words
they might find disturbing. This was the eminent merit of some
great popes: Gregory VII, Paschal II, Innocent II, Honorius
III, and so on. . . . It was a sign of the greatness of this age
that the powerful were willing to open their ears to such language. We cannot imagine a modern despot hearing such a
voice and not throttling it in the act and hurling its owner into
the darkest dungeon.''*[7]*

•

*The twofold element so crucial to all legitimate criticism of
the church is epitomized in the* Dialogue *of Saint Catherine
of Siena (1347–80). Having written that the ministers of the
church, good or bad, are always to be reverenced (no. 120),
Catherine at once inveighs against their evil lives (or was it
the "good life"?) — their injustice, their concubinage, their
gambling, their lack of pastoral zeal, their greed, their simony.
But this paradox is an ideal expression of the contrast between
what the minister represents and the manner in which he represents it: between the treasure itself and the "earthen vessel"
that contains it (see 2 Cor. 4:7).*

[6]   Not only do they not give what they are in duty bound to
give to the poor, but they rob them through simony and their
hankering after money, selling the grace of the Holy Spirit. Some
are so mean that they are unwilling to give to the needy the very
things I [i.e., God — here in *The Dialogue* God is addressing Cath-
erine] have given them freely so that they might give them to
you — unless their hands are filled [with money] or they are plen-
tifully supplied with gifts [in return]. They love their subjects for
what they can get from them, and no more. They spend all the
goods of the Church on nothing but clothes for their bodies.
They go about fancily dressed, not like clerics and religious, but
like lords or court lackeys. They are concerned about having

grand horses, many gold and silver vessels, and well-adorned homes. . . .

Sometimes they administer correction as if to cloak themselves in this little bit of justice. But they will never correct persons of any importance, even though they may be guilty of greater sin than more lowly people, for fear that these might retaliate by standing in their way or deprive them of their rank and their way of living. They will, however, correct the little people, because they are sure these cannot harm them or deprive them of their rank. Such injustice comes from their wretched selfish love for themselves. . . .

For when someone comes to ask their advice about usury, because they are guilty of the same sin and have lost the light of reason, the advice they give is darksome, tainted by the passion within their own souls. . . .

They are concerned about nothing but the grandeur of rank and nobility and wealth, about knowing polished rhetoric; and worse, they will recommend their candidate [for high ecclesiastical office] by saying he is good looking! . . . They ought to be searching out the humble poor folk who in their humility avoid high office, but instead they pick those who in their bloated pride go seeking promotions [*Catherine of Siena: The Dialogue,* trans. Suzanne Noffke (New York: Paulist, 1980), pp. 232–49].

*We must admit that Saint Catherine sometimes allowed herself to be carried away by passion. Some of her criticism of the cardinals may be too conditioned by her personal position in the extremely complex question of the Western Schism.*

*That the schism numbered saints on both sides is indicative of the fact that criticism in the church may at times make genuinely evangelical demands that are not necessarily historically viable at the moment, owing to the complexity of the human element in history. In such cases, these criticisms will express a long-term goal rather than an immediate demand. In view of the complexity of this historical situation in which Saint Catherine lived and wrote, as also because of the difficulty of her rhetorical style, we shall omit any further citations from her writings, apart from the following brief excerpt, which demonstrates the freedom of expression with which she addresses the pope:*

[7] I hope, by the goodness of God, my venerable Father, that you will be able to quench your great self-love, and cease to love yourself for your own sake, or your neighbor and God for your own sake, and do just the opposite. . . . I could wish that you would become a genuinely good shepherd. . . . If up to the present time you have not been sufficiently strong, I ask and conjure you now to play the brave man, toil indefatigably, follow Christ whose Vicar you are. Have no fear of the threat of the torments ·you may suffer or the rebellion that may rage around you. . . . Keep watch over the affairs of the Church, appoint good shepherds and decent governors of your cities. . . . Return to Rome. Delay no longer. Your delays have already been the occasion of great upheavals. Courage, Holy Father. No more negligence![8]

*The woman who calls the pope the "sweet Christ of earth" addresses him "on behalf of the Christ of heaven." No wonder that the biographer from whom these last citations are taken should observe: "Anyone familiar with the extravagance of the formulas today by the faithful, and even by bishops, when writing to the Holy See, will be disconcerted by Catherine's letter." Catherine was not the only woman who, despite the limitations imposed upon her as such, found in the gospel the necessary freedom to speak forthrightly to the popes in those difficult times. Saint Brigid of Sweden is an even more unusual case in the history of the church. Residing in Rome, in the Campo Marcio, from 1350 onward, she wrote in her native language, and her counsellors (especially a certain "Master Matthew") translated her words into Latin. Then she would review the Latin. Saint Brigid claims to be reporting visions, and the very words of the Blessed Virgin Mary. Surely there is nothing to be seen in this but the desperation into which the situation of the church had by then plunged good souls. The very harshness and injustice of some of the saint's declarations suffice to give the lie to the supernatural character of the "vision" in question. But Brigid's words abide, and they are words*

*of criticism — desperate words, and words which, even without
the nuances of which they were perhaps in need, produced
their effect.*

*The following was written about 1371. The words ad-
dressed by the Blessed Virgin to Saint Brigid are intended for
Pope Gregory XI, with whom the saint was personally ac-
quainted.*

[8]  I inform Pope Gregory that he must transfer his see to
Rome. The devil and certain advisers have persuaded him to
remain where he is — and this out of carnal love for his relatives
and friends, and out of worldly delight and consolation. But
since you wish to be sure of the will of God, hear the following.
Do you wish to have me for your Mother? Then return to Rome
at once, without any delay, at once. In March, or the beginning
of April at the latest, see that you are in the city, or at any rate
in Italy. And if you do not obey this, know that you shall never
more enjoy my words, nor any other visitation or consolation of
mine [Saint Brigid of Sweden, *Revelations,* IV, 140].

*Perhaps things were more complicated than this. Politics al-
ways is. And perhaps it was something more than "carnal
love" that kept the Pope away from Rome. But it is very important to be able to recognize the justice of a cause, without
being blinded by the lack of nuance that so frequently distorts
the defense of even a just cause. At all events, thanks to their
recognition of the justice of Catherine's and Brigid's cause,
the popes returned to Rome. In another vision, Christ himself
speaks:*

[9]  Pope Gregory XI, hear these words of mine. . . . Why am
I so hateful to you? Must you be so brazen and pretentious with
me? Your Curia of earth plunders my court of heaven. And you,
O prideful one, rob me of my sheep! . . . You misappropriate
the goods of my poor, distributing them, shamelessly, to your
rich! . . . Why? Why must the greatest pride, the most insatiable
greed, and the most abominable lechery reign in your court?
Yes, I discern even the horrid, snub snout of simony. And — as
if that were not enough — you steal from me! You snatch num-

berless souls from my care, dispatching straight to hell nearly all who surround you, there in your Curia! ... Begin at last to renew my Church. ... Is that Church a holy, venerable Mother? No, it is a bawdyhouse! Follow my will to the letter as I have manifested it to you. Else know that you shall surely stand condemned before all my heavenly court, by the present sentence of spiritual justice [Saint Brigid of Sweden, *Revelations,* IV, 142].

•

*The reader may well have noted, in the first of the passages from Saint Bernard that appear at the beginning of this anthology, that Bernard pronounces his powerful criticism of the church in a sermon on the Song of Songs. In doing so he is being quite faithful to an exegetical tradition of long standing. The celebrated ecclesiological expression "chaste whore" was coined as a vehicle for applying to the church both the prophets' Prostitute Jerusalem, and the Spouse of the Song of Songs. Later it was seen that the simultaneous application was further warranted by the geographical coincidence of pagan Rome (the "Babylon" of the New Testament) and Christian Rome or the See of Peter. For the fathers of the church this geographical circumstance becomes a matter of profound theological significance. No wonder, then, that criticism of the church so often appears in theological commentaries on the Song of Songs.*

*We have a good example of this in the following passage from William of Auvergne (died 1249), one day to become Bishop of Paris. One of the most important theologians of the thirteenth century, William composed, among other works, a commentary on the Song of Songs (1228, while he was still a teacher of theology). Here he applies to the church the passage in which the Spouse is likened to the "steeds of Pharaoh's chariots" (Song 1:8). The power of this mighty, glorious cavalry is the Holy Spirit. But then William surveys his times, and the tone of his language abruptly alters.*

**[10]** Today, obviously all of this has completely changed. The church now indeed resembles a battle chariot of Pharaoh — far more than one of God! It thunders toward the abyss of wealth and pleasure — yes, the abyss of sin. The wheels of the doctors of the church have fallen from their axle — Christ the axle of life, whom these teachers no longer resemble. . . . Today the chariot of the church no longer rolls forward, but retreats, for the horses have reared and fallen back. Strong horses are no longer chosen for the ministries of the church — only young colts, little nephews, who have neither the breast nor the shoulders to draw the chariot. Nay more, brute chargers have degenerated, falling prey to an intolerable lack of discipline. Headstrong, impatient, angry, they break the bridles and splinter the yoke. . . .

At the upper edge of a tunic gleams a collar. It is the adornment of that garment. So the doctors — by the gold of their knowledge and the jewelry of their virtues — ought to surpass all others, as the collar outshines the part of the vesture to which it is joined. But Christ is terribly poor, and his tunic old and warn — and the collar of the church is tin and tin plate today, and glass instead of gems!

How so? In the majority of the doctors and preachers today is neither truth nor virtue. Wisdom and doctrine have fled. . . . These men scarcely are poor collars indeed, who when they should speak out, are silent. Not only do they fail to adorn the garment. They rend and tear it. Their quarrels and coteries separate it from the head of the tunic. . . . Further: collars must cross, to prevent facile access to the breast. Otherwise the latter may lie open to lascivious, corrupting touches. . . . Then most of the doctors and prelates of our day are definitely décolletage [*antimonilia,* "countercollars"]. Instead of protecting the garment of the church from illicit contact, they expose it to the same. Like filthy pimps, they simply prostitute the church to any passer-by, and make their profit with her sin. And so Ezekiel (23:21) writes, "The Egyptians fondled your breasts, caressing your bosom." Or to use Jeremiah's words (2:16): "The sons of Memphis and Taphanes have violated you completely, from head to foot. . . . "

"You are all beautiful, my love, there is no blemish on you"? No, rather the dire prophecy of Isaiah has been accomplished in her: "God has left the daughter's head bald" (Isa. 4:17). In depriving her of the contemplation of doctrine and heavenly wisdom, he has shaved her head, and in her are the words of Jeremiah (3:3) fulfilled: "You have a harlot's shameless brow." God has deprived her of her eyes: "All her guardians have been struck blind. . . . Her cheeks are the color of earth, her bloodless lips match the stiffness of her face" (Isa. 56:10). "Sion's daughter has lost her loveliness" (Lam. 1:6). Truly can it be said of her what is written in the prophet Isaiah (6:1): "My beloved Babylon has become a terrible specter to me." God's beloved is the church, as long as the church does not depart from the footsteps of the fathers; but now it is changed into Babylon, on account of its ugliness, and because impure spirits dwell in her that frighten God himself. For who would not be filled with fright to see the church with the head of an ass, teeth of a wolf, snout of a hog, cheeks pale and frightful, neck of a bull, and everywhere a form so savage and terrible as to paralyze with horror anyone laying eyes on it? Who would not say and think, before such horrible degeneration, that this is Babylon, rather than the Church of Christ? Who would not say of it that it is a desert, and not the city of God? . . .

Because of this horrid monster—depraved, carnal Christians, who fill the church but who remain hidden and invisible to the rest of its members—the heretics call the church Babylon the Whore. And seeing such depraved Christians—who are such in name only—surely the heretics are right, so long as they do not apply that shameful name to all Christians indiscriminately. For this is no Bride, but a monster, terrible and savage. . . . Finding it in such a state, can we possibly say of it, "You are all beautiful, my love, there is no blemish on you"? [William of Auvergne, *Commentary on the Song of Songs,* chap. 28, no. 3].[9]

*A cognate biblical image of the church, likewise a common-place throughout the history of theology, has been that of Rahab, the prostitute "innkeeper of saints" (Gregory of Elvira), who received in her house and protected the explorers gone out in search of the Land of Promise, and was in turn rescued by them when her countrymen sought to wreak vengeance on her for her aid to the invaders. The application is first made*

*with a chronological distinction (first whore, then virgin), al-
luding to the passage from paganism to the church. Later it
comes to be made in a simultaneous sense as well. Or again,
the church is prefigured by Tamar, the prostitute who coha-
bited with Judah (a figure of Christ, in the allegorism of the
church fathers), and who therefore carried in her womb the
future heirs of the divine promise.*[10]

*As we read texts from Saint Bernard or Saint Catherine,
we note the importance of the theme of the poor in their
criticisms of the church. This same theme is present in the
hard words of another saint, Saint Bernard's predecessor and
a cardinal, Saint Peter Damian (1007–72). Peter Damian is
best known for his attack on the sexual vices of the clergy*
(Liber Gomorrhianus), *which he criticized in terms so harsh
that he had a falling out with the pope. But he was also a
tireless assailant of simony, ecclesiastical honors, and the mis-
use of church property. The first of the texts I shall cite must
be understood in the context of a primitive economic situation
in which anything like state "social welfare" is unknown. The
responsibility for emergency assistance to the poor therefore
falls on the church, in virtue of the gospel injunction. In this
text Saint Peter Damian simply applies his principle that
wealth comports not the right of exclusive possession, but the
obligation to administer one's wealth in others' behalf. Our
second passage is an attack on the obsequiousness of ecclesiastics toward secular princes for the purpose of obtaining
honors and worldly power. The saint regards this servility as
a form of simony.*

**[11]**   Daily, a meal with the princes, or a wedding banquet.
Daily, preparations for such. And the result? The means that
should be affording relief to the poor are squandered on behalf
of the providers of sumptuous repasts. The bishop ought to be
the distributor and steward of the poor. But it is others who
belch at his heaped-up table, while those whose bare necessities
are thus being consumed languish at the door, wasted by hunger
[Saint Peter Damian, *Apologia for His Episcopal Resignation*,
chap. 2 (*PL* 145:445)].

**[12]**   Of the many things that displease me in the bishops of today, the most intolerable is that some of them, craving church honors with a desire hotter than the vapors of Etna, thereupon enter the clientele of the powerful as shamefully as if they had been bought as slaves. In other words, their ambition is to possess churches; so they leave church affairs in the lurch. They would be placed above their fellow citizens; and so they stoop to conduct unworthy of a citizen. ... Who can bear the sight of it? Ecclesiastical positions today are awarded to one who, to further his Church career, turns his back on his own church![11] He cannot condescend to fulfill his duty to his own church—he is too busy gaining control of the government of another!

Small wonder, then, that such a one, given the opportunity, devotes himself to oily words of flattery with his lords, caressing them with soft adulation. Slyly he ferrets out the best ways to please them and win their good favor. Oh, he flutters his eyelashes, he bows and scrapes, and his words feign the ecstasy of a tranquil heart in the great presence; meanwhile he is on tenterhooks lest he fail to anticipate the least movement or whim of his lord, as if he were hanging on the lips of the very Sibyl. His lord commands, "Walk," and he flies. "Stay a bit!" He turns to stone. My, his lord has a fever! Depend on it, our ecclesiastic is bathed in sweat. Is the weather a little too warm for his lord? Our man suffers the dog days. But if the lord feels a little chill, the other's entrails are all ashiver. Is the master sleepy? His toady collapses in a heap. Has Milord enjoyed a fine meal? Prepare to hear the ecclesiastical belch. And so His Reverence neither says nor does anything of himself, but only what he thinks will please his master. Isaiah of old declared, of the like of these: "They say to the seers, 'Have no visions'; to the prophets, 'Do not descry for us what is right; speak flatteries to us, conjure up illusions.' Out of the way! Out of our path! Let us hear no more of the Holy One of Israel' " (Isa. 30:10–11).

Nor let them deny their simony, if out of ambition for office they behave as the clients of princes. ... [Saint Peter Damian, *Opusculum 22 contra Clericos Aulicos ut ad Dignitates Provehantur,* chap. 1 (*PL* 145:463-65)].

*It was during the pontificate of Eugene III (to whom Saint Bernard, as well, would one day address himself) that an*

*Augustinian canon, one Gerhoh (1093–1169), later Abbot of Reichersberg, wrote a treatise on the corruption of the church. Gerhoh was regarded by some as the most knowledgeable interpreter of the German theological tradition. The treatise is dedicated to the pope and is in the form of a commentary on Psalm 64: "O God, you deserve a hymn in Sion." The "hymn" is transformed by Gerhoh into a vehicle for his criticism of bishops who are constantly absent from their dioceses, or who devote themselves to intrigues or business dealings (commercial or military); or of nuns who sleep outside their convent (and postpone their monastic vows to the end of their lives); and he alleges that his fellow canons regularly do similar things. Here are a few paragraphs from this wearisome tractate:*

[13]  We write this treatise for the eyes of the Pope, that the Roman Curia—which, according to the testimony of Peter (1 Pet. 5:13), is the church in Babylon (Babylon being a metaphor for Rome)—may use caution, strive to shake off its Babylonian shame, and present itself without wrinkle or blemish, both itself and the whole church which it ought to govern. For what we today call the Roman Curia or Court, and used to call the Roman Church, is anything but without blemish! ...

... Kings and governors wish to command, not to be taught. Wherefore they have been known to murder witnesses of the truth. And even some shepherds (who are such in name and garb only, being ravening wolves within), contrary to the teaching of Peter, the supreme shepherd, and lording it over the clergy, murder the witnesses of the truth and deal with them as did Herod: first they cast them into prison, that they may not speak out publicly; then they have their throats cut. They manage to escape indictment for homicide, this is true; but they cannot escape the allegation of testicide: for it is one thing to kill a human being [as such], and another to kill a witness [as such]. You kill a human being by depriving him of his life. You kill a witness by depriving him of the opportunity to study and give witness, so that you may remain free to continue committing illicit things "licitly," inasmuch as no one any longer reproaches you with it. ...

How many who behave as Herod and Herodias! And how few reproach them with their behavior. Or — to cite some excellent examples: how many kings and princes sing as did David, yet how few repent as he! . . . Even the illiterate seek faithful trustees or administrators (see 1 Cor. 4:2), but how few of our administrators would dare to say with Paul that "men see in us only servants of Christ and dispensers of the mysteries of God" (1 Cor. 4:1); or, "Let us conduct ourselves in all things as servants of God, lest our ministry be censured" (2 Cor. 6:4). To be sure, many are concerned that their "ministry not be censured" — but they defend that ministry with swords and clubs, terror and threat, thus rendering it still more worthy of censure in the eyes of God and men [Gerhoh of Reichersberg, *Commentarium in Psalmos*, 64 (*PL* 194:9, 48, 112)].

*In another work by this same author,* On the Condition of the Church, *we read the following:*

**[14]**   The condition and face of the church are so miserable today that it is not easy to find a scripture passage to describe her. There is only the account of the woman of Israel in the time of the Judges who was raped to death all one night by the men of Gibeah (Judg. 19). . . . What wife is this, who has abandoned her father to become an Israelite's bride, but Holy Church, who has abandoned her father — the devil and the world — to become the bride of Christ? But how often this woman forsakes her husband to return to her father! The church does the same when she allows the love of Christ to grow cold in her heart and rejoins this world or its prince, the devil, in the house of incredulity or ill behavior. But her Bridegroom, Christ, calls her back each time by the voice of her shepherds and doctors, and through the outpouring of the Spirit of his love, stirring her old ardor and whispering: "Hear, O daughter, see, incline your head, and forget your people and your father's house, for the king is taken with your beauty" (Ps. 44:18). But the church dawdles here below on earth, among prideful and perverse men . . . and so is herself corrupted by their pride, as by their perverse thoughts and deeds.

And of all the times the church has ever had to suffer this

abuse at the hands of evil and corrupt men, it seems to me that the most shameful is the fornication to which she has been subjected today at the hands of this pack of unbridled simoniacs, who do nothing but assault her, slaking their evil impulses in her chastity.... Yes, of the church too we must say that her corruptors have so abused her, all night through (the hour of darkness), that she is on the point of death. Indeed, in many communities the fire of sacramental life, by which they could have fostered her life, has died out altogether—as the safety during the years of the Babylonian Captivity died out along with that life. For we hear that that fire was extinguished when Jason and Menelaus gained control of the high priesthood simply by purchasing it with gold [Gerhoh of Reichersberg, *On the Condition of the Church* (*PL* 194:1458–59)].

*Few writers in the history of the church have had more love for that church than the poet Dante (1265–1321). And few literary works are more ecclesiastical than Dante's* Divine Comedy. *The epic has been compared to a cathedral, or to a great theological* Summa *of the Middle Ages. Furthermore, many commentators would have it—as the presence of Beatrice and Virgil would seem to suggest—that the* Divine Comedy *echoes an autobiographical concern. Hell and purgatory would thus be more than eschatological situations; they would be actual moments in the life of the author. And here is another paradox: that no one has spoken more lovingly of the church, or more harshly of its leaders and institutions, than Dante. All parts of the poem provide its author with the opportunity for a protest—sometimes justified and sometimes not, in retrospect—but that protest is always the fruit of an unquestionable love for the church. Dante peopled hell and purgatory with cardinals "who must be regarded, sad though it be," as unclean, ravening wolves in the clothing of shepherds and clerics. While his personal criticism may be colored by the political struggles of his time, then, what interests us are his attacks on the situation, and very structure, of the church. "[It is in Rome] where every day Christ is bought and sold," he says (Paradise 17:51). After all:*

**[15]**   The church of Rome, through confounding in itself two modes of rule, falls in the mire, and defiles itself and its burden [*Purgatory* 16:127–29].

> *Later in the* Purgatorio *Dante paints the church as a chariot drawn by Christ. Then all in the scene changes. The chariot is transformed into a monster, and a whore (the Roman Curia) clambers aboard the transformed chariot and is seated. Dante describes the whore and the ensuing actions in the scene:*

Secure as a fortress on a high mountain, there appeared to me a dishevelled whore sitting upon the monster. She boldly leered around. And then, as if to guard her for himself, I saw a giant [the French monarchy] standing at her side. Now and again they kissed each other. But because she turned her lustful and roving eye on me, that fierce lover scourged her from head to foot. Then full of jealousy, and cruel with anger, he untied the monster from the tree and dragged it far away into the wood. Whore and monster alike were lost to my sight [*Purgatory* 32:148–60].

> *Dante excoriates Pope Nicholas III, whom he finds buried in hell:*

**[16]**   Tell me now, how much treasure did our Lord require of Saint Peter before he placed the keys in his hands? Surely he demanded nothing but "follow me." Nor did Peter or the others take gold or silver from Matthias, when he won by lot the post that guilty soul [Judas] had lost. Therefore, stay here, for you are rightly punished, and guard well your ill-gotten money. . . . And were it not that even now I shrink because of reverence for the mighty keys that you once held while in your life above, the language that I use would be much harsher, because your avarice afflicts the world, and trampling down the good, exalts the bad. The evangelist had shepherds like you in mind when he saw her that sits on the waters [Rome, the church] committing fornication with the kings — that woman who was born with seven heads, and from the ten horns had argument, so long as the way of virtue pleased her husband [the pope]. You have set up a god of gold and silver: How do you differ from idolaters, save that they worship one, and you a hundred? Ah Constantine! How evil was the seed sown not by your conversion, but by the dowry the first rich father once received from you! [*Inferno* 19:89–117].

*Now in Paradise, the poet is addressed by Saint Peter himself, who comes forth from a select company in the celestial choir and says these words:*

[17]   If I change color, marvel not; for, as I speak, you will see these others change color as well. He who on earth usurps my place [Boniface VIII], my place, my place, which is vacant in the presence of the Son of God, has made of my cemetery a sewer of blood and filth. . . . The Bride of Christ was not nurtured on my blood, and that of Linus and of Cletus, to be used for gain of gold, but for the acquisition of this glad state. . . . It was not our intention that part of the Christian people should sit on the right hand of our successors, and part on the other; nor that the keys which were entrusted to me should become an emblem on a standard borne to make war on the baptized; nor that I should be made a figure on a seal to venal and mendacious privileges, which make me blush and feel hot shame. Rapacious wolves, in garb of shepherds, are seen from here on high throughout the pastures [*Paradise* 27:19–55].[12]

•

*In Dante's words, as in those of Saint Bernard, above, we have an allusion that gradually came to be a* locus communis *where criticism of the church was concerned: the pejorative notion of the "Constantinian," or worldly power, of that church. It may be worthwhile to pause here for a moment to examine the currency of this concept in ecclesiastical literature. Far from being the monopoly of a few writers or of later times, the allusion attaches to demands for reform reaching back to the time of Constantine himself. This is what strikes us in the following words of Saint Hilary of Poitiers, written in 364. Hilary was the first Christian writer to upbraid the Emperor*

*Constantine. He ends a lengthy composition of his by likening Constantine to the emperors who had persecuted the church (Nero, Decius, and so on) — inasmuch as, for Saint Hilary at any rate, power harms the church more than persecution has ever done. And so Hilary says of the emperor:*

[18]    He does not impale us with his sword. No, he strokes our belly. He does not confiscate our goods, and thereby give us life — he enriches us, that we may die. He does not cast us into dungeons, thereby setting us on the path to freedom — he imprisons us in the honors of his palace. . . . He showers priests with honors, so that there will be no good bishops. He builds churches, that he may dismantle the faith [*PL* 10:580ff.].

*But Hilary not only upbraids the emperor. He also addresses the church of his time, in a book against the Arians addressed to Bishop Auxentius of Milan. The work opens with the following paragraphs:*

[19]    How painful to have to contemplate so much effort in our time, so many foolish notions calculated to further the cause of God with merely human resources! See the toil to defend the church of Christ by the machinations of worldly ambition! You bishops who are of this mind, I have some questions for you. Of what worldly means did the apostles avail themselves to proclaim the gospel? What earthly powers furthered their preaching of Christ, as they went about nearly the whole world, rescuing it from idolatry and establishing in it the worship of the one true God? Did they who, after being scourged, sang hymns to God in their prison cells, regard themselves as dignitaries of imperial households? Did Paul gather a church unto Christ by way of imperial edicts--he who regarded himself as a mere spectacle in a theater? Did he bask in the patronage of Nero? Or was he perhaps defended by Vespasian or Decius, whose hatred of us watered the faith that now has sprouted and flourished? And think you that the keys of the kingdom of heaven were not in the hands of all of the missionaries who maintained themselves by manual labor, who met their flocks secretly, and who plied land and sea to reach the towns, villages, and countryside of

almost the entire world, flying in the face of the laws of the Senate and emperors? Or think you that the power of God was not made manifest, against all human raging, in the fact that, the more Christ was under interdict, the more he was preached?

But today! — what a sight! The divine faith is placed under human protection, while the power of Christ is accused of impotence, and the ambition of power waxes sleek on his Name. The church, which once spontaneously believed — when it was in prison and exile — now obliges belief by threats precisely of prison or exile! . . . She basks in the world's adulation who can only belong to Christ if the world holds her in contempt. A comparison between the traditional church, lost today, and the one we see now, fairly cries to heaven [Hilary of Poitiers, *Contra Arianos*, 3–4 (*PL* 10:610–11)].

•

*In 1307, in anticipation of the Council of Vienne, which was to convene five years later, Bishop William Durandus wrote his* On the Manner of Celebrating the Council and Reforming the Church. *William's interminable list of proposals and recommendations incidentally presents quite a concrete image of church life at that time, ranging as it does over the widest possible variety of persons (laity, friars, nuns, cardinals, and so on) and of situations — he recommends that bishops be forbidden to absent themselves from their dioceses for more than three weeks at a time, that houses of prostitution not be built so near the papal residence or the homes of curial officials that it might be suspected that that is where church money goes, and so on and on. William likewise proposes that, in conformity with the dispositions of the Council of Carthage and the practice of an earlier pope, the Roman pontiff style himself merely Bishop of the First Church, rather than High Priest or Prince of Priests. He further recommends that, in the matter of priestly celibacy, the custom of the Eastern church be adopted as being more in keeping with the practice of the apostles. The author is a devout Christian, convinced of the importance of the good example of the hierarchy for the cred-*

*ibility of the church.*[13] *Hence he does not hesitate, on occasion,*
*to reproach the Roman Curia. Nor does he mince any words.*

**[20]**  Balaam's ass, with her human voice, is a study in contrast
with a foolish prophet. And we behold the same today in the
boundless stupidity and immorality being perpetrated in the
church of God by persons of the church. Instead of being light
for others, as they ought, they provoke the contempt even of
persons not versed in the things of God, who often have a better
sense of such matters than they, and who therefore strive to
correct them and deter them from their godless ways. Who can
help but think of Augustine's description of the "unlearned who
teach the learned, and the laity the clergy"? [part 1, no. 1].

True, kings and pontiffs are human, and can readily
fall. . . . But this does not afford the pope a license to sin by
claiming ownership of the see of Peter. Not even Peter owned
that see! . . . And of course we all know the saying: "The wider
the hug, the weaker the squeeze." Thus it is that popes, although
invested with more dignity than others, are not always more
abreast of the requirements of a given situation, in view of the
detailed information required for conduct of business, as Saint
Gregory once observed . . . [ibid., no. 3].

Wise though one be, one must not disdain to give ear to the
great wisdom that may be on the lips of a little one. As Saint
Paul wrote, if something be revealed to the least, then let the
greatest hold their tongues [part 2, pref.].

It ought to be considered whether, in the College of Cardinals, as in the episcopal bodies and wherever else it might be
suitable, it would not be well to maintain the usage [of the
primitive church], based on natural law, of common ownership
of all things. How much anxiety for the accumulation of wealth
would be eliminated! It would also be well for cardinals, bishops,
and so on, not to be allowed to hold more than one benefice,
as they thereby give bad example, and occasion a wastefulness
as harmful to their souls as to their churches [ibid., no. 2].

Simony has corrupted the universal church and all its peoples,
and this in the highest degree. The means taken to counter it
are of no avail, since simony is as publicly practiced in the Roman Curia as if it were no sin to commit it — or as if paying for

a benefice after receiving it were not the same as doing so be-
forehand [ibid., no. 20].

The church of Rome stands as a mirror and example to all.
And as no mirror must be stained, or rusty, so the church must
take care that nothing reprehensible be observed in her. After
all, a headache makes you hurt all over!...And: "Shake the
pillars, down comes the house."

Let us remember what Our Lord told the scribes and Pharisees. [There follows an extensive citation from Matthew 23.]
For, according to Saint John Chrysostom, these same words can
be applied to the prelates and priests of our day, who impose
strict morals on the people, while their own morality is not even
average. Thus they appear righteous, judging by their words, but
are not so, judging by their deeds. Meanwhile, the Psalmist asserts that the eyes of the servants (those below, the laity) are
on the hands (the works) of their masters (their bishops and
superiors); and that the eyes of the handmaid are on the hands
of her lady, the Roman Church.... And this is true especially
in the case of the pope, who occupies the place of him who
"began to *act* and to speak," and who, to the multitude who
followed him, gave bodily nourishment, and not merely the food
of his teaching [part 3, no.1].[14]

*With all the more vigor as his language is the more concrete,
Henry of Langenstein (1325–97), Vice-Chancellor of the University of Paris, worked with Jean de Gerson and other well-
known writers in an attempt to end the Western Schism. In a
work titled* Council of Peace, *he criticizes certain usages prev-
alent in the church of his time:*

[21]  Once more—to what end, and to what profit of the
church, are all the magnificence of its princes, and all the prideful pomp of its bishops and other prelates, as if they knew not
that they are men? And to what end the aberration by which
one churchman will hold two to three hundred ecclesiastical
benefices? Is it not obvious that this is harmful to worship, that
it impoverishes the churches, that she is deprived of worthy men,
and that the faithful are given bad example?...Really, now,
must dogs, horses, birds, and all the rest of the superfluous

retinue of ecclesiastics devour the patrimony of the church today while Christ's poor go hungry? . . . Judge for yourselves whether it be right that, time and again, books or lands or buildings belonging to the church are sold off to pay taxes imposed by the bishops on the clergy! . . .

And why is the sword of the church—I refer to the sword of excommunication—so lightly and cruelly drawn against the poor, in paltry matters like petty debts? Why so lengthy a lawsuit over so trifling an amount of money? Why not put an end to such prolixity in court proceedings, which eventually can only bleed the poor?

How comes it that certain prelates lease their temporal and spiritual jurisdiction to mighty tyrants for a sum of money? This only redounds to the detriment of the church, the prejudice of justice, and the oppression of the poor. Bishops, abbots, and monks today are ministers of finance, not of Christ, as they struggle with might and main to master the world of princely courts, legal courtrooms, and worldly parliaments.

Again: what does it mean that nearly all bishops, prelates, and pastors today are named by the pope, instead of the most suitable and best known individuals of each country being elected? Were the latter the usage, men foreign to these lands, and strange to their customs, languages, and habits of life, would no longer preside over the churches. Why must young striplings, the sons of the high and mighty, be placed in the forefront of ecclesiastical dignity, while clerics renowned for their life and teaching are ranked below them? . . . Must the church be governed after the manner of the world, rather than precisely in a manner contrary to worldly usage? Scripture says: "Conform not to the usages of this world" . . . [*J. Gersonii Opera Omnia* (Amberes, 1706), Appendix, vol. 2, cols. 837–38].

*In the same volume in which the foregoing citation appears, once more in the second volume of the Appendix (at column 885), we find a text of the Cardinal Chamberlain Pedro de Aliaco showing that feelings like those of Gerson were known to many bishops, and even to the College of Cardinals. In chapter 1 of Aliaco's* Recommendations on the Need for Reform in the Church, *we find:*

[22] How often we beg God in the church that he would teach us to condemn the things of earth and love the things of heaven. Now, to condemn the things of earth means to hold them in lower esteem than the things of Christ. Then how comes it that Christ is so condemned in the Roman Curia, and gold is preferred? Why is the good of unity in the universal church forgotten, although it is the good that all should seek — and all the more intensely, the more exalted the dignity of the seeker? ...

•

*In 1417, on the occasion of the Council of Constance, Nicholas of Clemanges, the Archdeacon of Paris and a doctor of theology, published his treatise,* On the Condition of the Corruption of the Church, *in which he analyzes the situation of schism in the church as principally owing "to the vices of the ministers of the church, whose legacy and property ought to have been Christ." The treatise is without a doubt the harshest of the works cited in the present anthology. It attacks the actual, concrete policy of the popes, which to the mind of the author was simply worldly, ambitious, selfish, even tyrannical. Every page is a veritable diatribe, and most unpleasant reading. But the author maintains that God must first humble the church before God can correct it.*

[23] Who could describe such insatiable greed, transcending the lust for gain of all the world of commerce? What provocation, what incitement to injustice to the eyes of all of the laity! ... Let us examine the progress of this infamous plague, which sickens its victim from head to foot. After all, one cannot serve lords as opposed as God and mammon. All the diligence used in the service of the one will inevitably result in the neglect of the other [2]. The spirit of ecclesiastics has been infected by a great abundance of worldly things, and by their immense avarice ... so that they have had to serve three tyrants: Luxury, ... Pomp, ... and Ambition. ... And inasmuch as no ordinary revenue would enable a person to carry out the injunctions of these three rapacious harpies, our churchmen have had to seek other perquisites ... [3].

Thus the popes—to begin with them—have transformed all their superiority of primacy and authority into a superiority of power and a passion to lord it over others. And deeming the revenue of the Roman See and the patrimony of Peter (which once was far more extensive than that of many kings, who now have seen to its abridgment) inadequate to satisfy their longing to be more important than anyone else, they have begun to appropriate the milk and wool of the flocks of others [4] . . . and to flood their curia with rivers of gold that stream from all sides. And thus (in addition to what we have just said concerning the elections) they have deprived their diocesan clergy and patrons of the faculty of offering candidates and of the liberty of conferring and disposing of benefices, forbidding them under pain of anathema that they should grant anyone any benefice if that person is not the one to whom the pope has promised it. . . . This is the cause of the ubiquitous appearance of so many immoral, ignorant priests, whose manner of life is a scandal to their people. And this is why so much anticlericalism is on the lips of the people. This is why so much division prevails in the ecclesiastical order, occasioning remarks that would make the clergy blush with shame if they knew shame. But their face is hard. They cannot blush. . . . Once, nothing was regarded as more worthy of veneration than the priestly state. Today nothing is more abject and contemptible [7].

Furthermore, the popes have added to this a whole series of taxes and tributes on persons and churches, . . . appointing tax collectors for all the provinces—hard men, who know how to gouge money out of you. . . . Incapable of mercy, they can wring gold from stones. And [the popes] have actually conferred upon them the authority to anathematize prelates and excommunicate faithful unless payments are made on time. . . . How many complaints this occasions on the part of poor ministers of the church, whom we hear and see performing their ministry under an unbearable yoke—yes, nearly starving! Behold the source of all *suspensio a divinis* [suspension of the right to celebrate the Eucharist], all interdicts, and all these wildly exaggerated anathemas, which ought to be imposed only very rarely and for the most horrible crimes . . . but which today are imposed for the least offense, if indeed for any at all. No one fears them any longer. They are become the universal laughingstock [8–9].

I must omit many things if I am ever to emerge from this morass — for example, all the fraud committed in the Roman Curia, all the deceit, all the calumny, all the court proceedings corrupted by those money-chasers, all the trampling on the rights of the innocent, all the venal judges, all the power of gold to overthrow justice, all the difficulty a poor person has in obtaining justice from a rich adversary. . . . It is no longer the shepherd who enters by the gate of the sheepfold, but the thief who climbs in, anywhere he will. And an impartial observer who could distinguish between them would find far more thieves than shepherds in the church! Surely Christ's words are applicable to them: " 'My house is a house of prayer.' But you have made it a den of thieves!" [10–12].

As for the cardinals who surround the pope, if an artist wished to erect a monument to pride, he could wish for no better model than a cardinal, with all his pompous words and arrogant gestures. They come from the lower clergy, and have become so puffed up with the pomp and splendor of the Apostolic See, . . . they have stitched their phylacteries so broad, that they despise, and all but demand the worship of, the primates, patriarchs, and bishops (whom they like to call "bishoplings") . . . [13].

And finally, before taking leave of the curia, I cannot pass over in silence the abominable adultery of the pope and his brethren with the princes of this world. For in order to safeguard and stabilize their dominions, or rather their tyranny, which the whole world so rightly despises, . . . they have trimmed and molded themselves so as to capture the favor and friendship of all temporal princes, accustoming themselves to imitating the latter in their behavior and mentality . . . [18] [Ed. Fco. Clousier, Paris, 1671].

*From the pope and cardinals the author moves on (nos. 20–28) to the bishops ("Why are they blamed for being absent from their dioceses when their presence does more harm than good?"), chaplains and canons, monks, the mendicant orders, and nuns. And he concludes:*

[24]   Compare this kind of life with that of our early fathers. You will be comparing mud with gold. We seem to have come to the end of the affair—like the feet of that statue of Nebuchadnezzar, which, from its head of gold downward, was fashioned of less and less noble metals, silver, then iron, until finally his feet were fashioned of clay, and clay crumbles. This is where we are now. . . .

But let no one think that, with all that I have said about ecclesiastics, I accuse all without exception. I know very well that he did not lie who said: "I have besought the father for you, that you fail not." Nor am I ignorant of the fact that, in all of the ecclesiastical states, there may be some, even many, good, righteous, and innocent persons, who are innocent of all the evils I have described. But so great is the abundance of the wicked in all of these offices that I really know not whether one in a thousand sincerely performs all that his profession demands . . . [37–39] [Clousier edition].

*It may be that some of the language of this last author is inspired by the tragedy of the Avignon Schism. But neither can we deny that, eventually, the key word in the demands made of the church by many of our writers—the word "reform"—was to become the hue and cry of Luther's break with Rome. The criticism of the twelfth century was heard, and this contributed to the splendor of the church of the thirteenth century. But the criticism of the fourteenth and fifteenth century fell on deaf ears, and its rejection paved the way for Luther's break with the church.[15] The Council of Trent, then, in the opinion of many historians, came too late.[16] It did not succeed in healing the rift in the church. It only stanched the hemorrhage. But we must still ask when (or even whether) the Council of Trent would ever have been held, had it not been for so many prophetic voices who dared call for it, publicly and aloud, over the objections of the Roman Curia. It was a time when someone as loyal to the papacy as Saint Ignatius Loyola could declare that "only three things" were needed "for a pope to change the world: the reform of his own person, the reform of his house and household, and the reform of the Curia of Cardinals."[17] Another example comes from the pen of Peter*

*of Leyden, the prior of the Carthusians of Cologne. About
1530, he published the minor works (Opuscula) of Denis the
Carthusian. Peter of Leyden added an unexpected foreword
in the form of an open letter to Pope Clement VII. Here are
some extracts:*

[25]   I address you not only in my name, but in that of many,
if not all, of your children. What we ask is called a "reform of
the church." There are many things that ought not only to invite
you to undertake such a reform, but fairly to thrust you to it.
Perhaps I should declare what it is that moves us, and all those
of us who seek to be devout, to make this request of you, and
why we dare ask you for an ecumenical council for the repair
of the integrity of the church. . . .

Surely it is your duty to avoid a scandal among the humble
people. But what is on the lips of all the people today but that
the pope does not dare to convoke a council? That "His Holiness" does not want conversion? That the Vicar of Christ is
unwilling to abandon his pomp and circumstance? That the Sovereign Pontiff will not correct the lasciviousness of the
clergy? . . . Do you doubt that we are wounded by all these slan-
ders, we who have a different opinion of you? Do you doubt
that these calumnies scandalize those who, not knowing you,
believe them all? Though there were nothing to be gained but
the elimination of this actual scandal, through a demonstration,
in deeds and not in words, that it is unjust to think this of you,
and a lie that the curia is this greedy and lustful — by this alone
would God be adequately glorified. . . .

Many will be surprised that an individual monk should address Your Holiness in this manner. But I think that, on this
point, neither am I moved by a presumption of grandeur, nor
you by the conceit of pride. And as Your Holiness's excellency
does not spurn a son, neither does the humility of my littleness
fear to approach a father. Who would dare to forbid a son to
approach his father? Who could be annoyed with a son for loving
his father, or because he made suggestions to him or counseled
him in a matter of common interest? Why should I fear annoying
anyone if we are all your children and members of the church,
and if what I ask is the health of the whole body — health for

the brethren, health for your sick children?

What is not contaminated in the church, corrupted, perverted? The church is ill, from the soles of her feet to the crown of her head.... We need pay no regard to the calumnies of heretics. Think only of the detriment of so many souls, the seduction of so many simple ones, the lack of obedience, the little virtue of the people, the corrupt customs of the upper classes, the unbridled luxury of the clergy, the detestable pomp of the bishops, the petulancy of the monks, the arrogance of the common people, the idle, corrupt, and yes, perilous life of the rich.... And these things move many persons of good will to withdraw from obedience to Rome and from the truth of the church. Anticlericalism increases steadily, monasteries are deserted, and all the while the life of the entire clergy is so scandalous as not to merit the least esteem....

And what would [the emperor do] should he see that the vicar of Christ, with a view to reforming the church, is capable of despising wealth and glory, and bending low enough to subject himself, together with the cardinals, who stand in such need of reform, to an ecumenical council? ... While the articles of faith already pronounced by the church cannot be changed, nevertheless—as times and men change—it becomes necessary to change, adjust, or altogether abandon things now in place, even when they are the object of religious observance [Petrus von Leyden, introd. to *Opera Dionisii Cartusiani* (Cologne edition), 33:9–12].

•

*I have referred to Saint Ignatius Loyola. Let us recall that there appeared in Alcalá in 1503, in the translation of Fray Ambrosio de Montesinos, the* Life *of Christ, written by "a Carthusian." This was the work that was to achieve renown as the book that converted Ignatius as he lay convalescing in his birthplace near Azpeitia from a battle wound, desperate for some reading, any reading, to while away the weary hours. The Carthusian's work contains a chapter (chapter 68) entitled "On the Ambition and Disordinate Greed for Honor and Other Defects of the Clergy and Religious." Now, must not*

*Ignatius have felt himself to be included in this criticism? After all, he was technically a cleric (having received the tonsure at about twelve years of age, probably with a view to his future economic security, in accordance with a pernicious custom of the age). And although the later life of "Gentleman Iñigo" evinced precious little behavior in conformity with his "clerical" state, we know that Ignatius was aware of being a member of that state, since on one occasion—that of a court proceeding in Azpeitia—he had sought to appeal to it in order to escape the civil jurisdiction. Thus it is reasonable to suppose that he felt himself included in the object of the denunciations of the Carthusian. What magnificent fruit borne by criticism— the actual conversion of a person, be it only of a single individual! Here are the words of "the Carthusian":*

[26]   Some inordinate lovers of these honors, their self-love deceiving their reason, determine to procure them under pretense of winning souls—of better serving the salvation of others. . . .

Other evils flow from ambition. The first is that its victims so frequently seek, through their own efforts as well as through the offices of others, to be promoted to and installed in ecclesiastical charges without having been called to them by God's grace.

The second evil is that, all too frequently, one's friends according to the flesh are preferred, in the conferral of benefices, to others more virtuous and more worthy. . . .

The fourth evil is that scarcely anyone is found to be content with a single benefice, and this attitude redounds to the prejudice and detriment of the rest of the clergy. . . . We know of a certain Master Philip, who, having held various prebends in his life, was unwilling to abandon them even on his deathbed. But shortly after his death he appeared to his bishop, William, to tell him that God had condemned him on that account. . . . And so, in all that we have said, we have a glimpse of the extent and gravity of the danger of the state in which clerics live today, and we see what scandals are occasioned by these persons. With the patrimony of the Cross of Christ they maintain their concubines, feed their dogs, and trap out their horses so very elegantly.

... And how much persecution they occasion and stir up against Holy Church ... !

Never has the devil persecuted the church as he does today. Our adversary Lucifer persecuted the infant church by the hand of tyrants. He persecuted it in its adolescence by the hand of heretics. But now that it abides at the summit of its prosperity, he persecutes it by illicit movements and inordinate desires, idle waste and evil desires. This is what we see in the church today. Nowhere is there such pride, such ambition and immorality, as among clerics and prelates. Wherefore Saint Jerome says: "Pride is a vice peculiar to the demons or to women. The vices of the flesh are proper to brute beasts. Greed is the vice of merchants. But all three have combined to make up that monster of horrid and unsightly aspect, clerical vice."[18]

*If the great Tridentine reform was indeed "too late," this is all the greater pity in view of the fact that texts like the one I have just cited did at last produce their effect, and at the very highest level of the church. In 1522, the last non-Italian pope before John Paul II, Adrian VI, dispatched a legate named Chieregati to the Diet of Ratisbon with some startling instructions. He bore the words of a pope who spoke of the condition of the papacy and the Roman Curia in tones of utmost severity, and his words were as sincere as they were uncompromising. Adrian VI instructed Chieregati as follows:*

[27]  You are also to say that we frankly acknowledge that God permits this persecution of His Church on account of the sins of men, and especially of prelates and clergy. . . . Holy Scripture declares aloud that the sins of the people are the outcome of the sins of the priesthood; therefore, as Chrysostom declares, when our Savior wished to cleanse the city of Jerusalem of its sickness, He went first to the Temple to punish the sins of the priests before those of others, like a good physician who heals a disease at its roots. We know well that for many years things deserving of abhorrence have gathered round the Holy See; sacred things have been misused, ordinances transgressed, so that in everything there has been a change for the worse. Thus it is not surprising that the malady has crept down from

the head to the members, from the popes to the hierarchy.

We all, prelates and clergy, have gone astray from the right way, and for long there is none that has done good. ... Therefore, in our name, give promises that we shall use all diligence to reform before all things the Roman Curia, whence, perhaps, all these evils have had their origin; thus healing will begin at the source of sickness. ... We desire to wield our power not as seeking dominion or means for enriching our kindred, but in order to restore to Christ's bride, the Church, her former beauty, to give help to the oppressed, to uplift men of virtue and learning, above all, to do all that beseems a good shepherd and a successor of the blessed Peter [cited in Ludwig Pastor, *The History of the Popes* (St. Louis: Herder, 1923), 9:134–35].

*Adrian VI was unable to carry out his reform. His pontificate was too brief, and curial opposition too dogged. Although he pleads for patience in the document just cited, as he is aware that not everything can be done at once, even citing Aristotle to that effect ("Any sudden change is very dangerous for a community") — nevertheless he collided with the Roman Curia. Further, his command of Italian was poor. To the mind of the cardinals, it was unbearably cruel of the pope to refuse to practice nepotism, and they coined an expression that was to achieve common currency in its time: "Rome," sighed their eminences, "is no longer Rome!" Nevertheless the seed planted by Adrian germinated, and years later, in 1537, a commission of cardinals (including Contarini, Caraffa, Sadoleto, and Pole), together with a number of bishops, addressed a "memorial" to Paul III calling for the reform of the curia and echoing all of the accents with which we are now familiar. Pastor writes:*

[28] The memorial points out as the root of all ecclesiastical abuses the reckless exaggeration of the Papal authority by unscrupulous canonists. ... From this source [excessive papal power], as it were *ex equo Trojano*, had issued all the abuses which had brought the Church to the verge of destruction and

on themselves an evil repute among unbelievers [Ludwig Pastor, *The History of the Popes* (St. Louis: Herder, 1923), 11:166].

*The memorial then goes on to criticize excessive concern for one's family in the admittance of candidates to holy orders and in the conferral of benefices; it also criticizes the lack of care exercised by religious in tending to the good of souls. It concludes:*

We have satisfied our consciences, not without the greatest hope of seeing, under your pontificate, the Church of God restored to a fair and dovelike purity and to inward unity, to the eternal glory of your name. You have taken the name of Paul. We hope that you will imitate his charity. He was chosen as an instrument to carry Christ's name to the heathen; you, we hope, have been chosen to revive in our hearts and deeds that name long since forgotten among the heathen and by us the clergy, to heal our sickness, to unite Christ's sheep again in one fold, and to avert from our heads the wrath and already threatening vengeance of God [Pastor, *History of the Popes*, 11:169; for a more extensive citation, see A. Ravier, *Ignace de Loyola fonde la Compagnie de Jésus* (Paris, 1974), p. 34].

*Nor were these accents destined for oblivion. For example, in his address at the opening of the second session of the Council of Trent, Cardinal Pole spoke as follows:*

[29]   If we fail to recognize all this, in vain do we embark upon the Council—and in vain do we invoke the Holy Spirit, whose first entry into the human soul is by way of the condemnation of man, "to convict the world of sin" (John 16:9). Until this Spirit has condemned us in our own eyes, we shall not be able to say that he has entered within us; nor indeed will he enter there if we refuse to turn our eyes upon our own sins [*Acta Concilii Trident.*, 4/1:550-51].

*And in the same tone, a critical one, without a solitary note of triumphalism, Cardinal de Lorena closed the council:*

They have the right to demand of us the cause of this wild, raging tempest. And whom are we to accuse, my brother bishops? . . . This storm has arisen because of us, Reverend Fathers. . . . "Let judgment begin with the house of the Lord" (1 Pet. 4:7), and "let them be purified who bear the Lord's vessels" (Isa. 52:11) [ibid., 9:163].

*However belatedly, then, criticism has finally borne fruit, and the church has taken a giant step forward in history. With that fact acknowledged, let us now broaden our reflections for a moment. Let us step back from our story and view these seething centuries as a whole.*

*1. The authors of nearly all of the criticisms I have cited have been irreproachable ecclesiastics, some of them canonized saints. I deliberately omitted many other pages of literature—Erasmus's* Praise of Folly, *for example, which is incomparably more brilliant in style, more incisive, and less boring than some of the paragraphs above. Or there is Liutprand of Cremona's* Antapodosis, *on the tenth-century popes; in that work's roguish coarseness may lurk a considerable dose of reprisal, it is true, even on the part of a bishop. Or—to cite a Spanish example, we could have quoted some of the ingenious, pricking verses of Rimado de Palacio, or again of Pero López de Ayala, which would come to be used in some of the songs of Paco Ibáñez.*

*I have deliberately excluded all of these. What interests me here is not the brilliance, nor even always the total justice of criticism of the church—but the legitimacy of its intent, so well reflected in a letter addressed by Petrarch to Francesco Bruni: "Nec homines accusare propositum fuit, sed Ecclesiae statum flere." ("Our intent has been not to accuse individuals, but to bewail the state of the church.")*[19]

*2. It may be useful to note that in none of the authors cited thus far do we find a fear of scandalizing the people with criticisms of the church. On the contrary, many of the authors recognize that the people are already scandalized, sheerly by the facts. Today we sometimes hear, "Simple folk don't suspect these things. Better not say anything. We might harm their faith." This often becomes a pretext for discrediting a criticism, as well, so that we feel no obligation to examine it and perhaps mend our ways. This is not to deny that people have very different "stomachs," or that different times offer different opportunities, and it would be obtuse of us to ignore this. But I am convinced that realism and awareness are multiplied a thousand times in a world plagued by the media, where people can live in shining innocence no longer, but, on the contrary, are bombarded by countless representations of the church, frequently one-sided and distorted, coming from outside that church.*

*3. And finally, it will be fitting to underscore the fact that all of these persons spoke and wrote in a historical time that antedated the age of individual rights, democracy, and free speech. The fact that under tyrannical and feudal regimes they could speak in this way in the church, when outside the church criticism was limited to buffoonery, transformed that church into an oasis of evangelical freedom, and lent credibility to its gospel despite the counter-witness of so many ecclesiastics. Criticism in the church bestows credibility on the church when it becomes a sign of that "eschatological instance" of which the church is the depository—that "not yet" which forbids the church to install itself in any situation as if it were the "already," the altogether present, of the reign of God. The sign of the gospel will not leave the church in peace, will not "leave it alone." But if, God forbid, despite the victory of the Enlightenment and critical awareness, the situation were to be reversed, and free speech were to become impossible precisely in the church, while not impossible outside the church, the resultant scandal would prevent people from recognizing the strength of the gospel in the church, and thus the credibility of the church would be diminished.*

*On the periphery of all these considerations—and resuming our theme—the best proof of the seriousness of the Catholic reform, at least where personal conduct is concerned, is the change we observe in the panorama of criticism after Trent. The saints of the baroque period do not register the displeasure with the church that we have encountered in some of the saints of the Middle Ages. There remain, nevertheless, structural problems, such as the lack of freedom on the part of the*

*bishops, product of a reaction to the various forms of "Gal-*
*licanism" universally pursued by the monarchs of Europe. But*
*these problems were outweighed by the experience of a hostility*
*"on the outside," and a corresponding need for self-defense.*
*The church must assert its identity, it was felt, in the face of*
*the attacks and the split of Protestantism. These attacks by*
*"other churches" inspire in persons of the post-Tridentine*
*church, including saints, more of a desire to defend themselves*
*than a concern for reform. This must go in the debit column*
*of the Catholic balance sheet after Luther's break. The inertia*
*that resisted the cry for a reform that finally materialized will*
*of course outlast Trent. And human sinfulness will endure.*
*Saint Vincent de Paul will have excellent reason to exclaim*
*that "the greatest enemy of the church is the clergy, owing to*
*their indolence," or "I fear lest this damnable traffic in bishops*
*call down the wrath of God upon this Kingdom."[20] Indeed it*
*is almost as if Trent's thrust for behavioral renewal somehow*
*checked itself for a while, in order to release it at some later*
*moment—for example, with the famous bull of Innocent XII,*
Romanum Decet Pontificem, *in which that pope finally en-*
*gages in a limited amount of self-criticism and reforms him-*
*self. Innocent accepted as incumbent on himself the*
*obligations imposed on other ecclesiastics by the canons for-*
*bidding bishops to use church property to fill their relatives'*
*coffers, and suppressed all the posts (civil, military, or eccle-*
*siastical) that had habitually been consigned as sinecures to*
*the relatives of the reigning pontiff. If the pope has poor rel-*
*atives, he may not render them more assistance than he offers*
*the rest of the poor. In fact, even if a papal relative were to*
*be elevated to the purple on the strength of his merits, and not*
*through the practice of nepotism, his emoluments are estab-*
*lished in advance, and the pope is not to add to them.*

*It will be worthwhile to cite the introduction, at any rate,*
*of this tiresome document, as it calls for what we today would*
*call a papal "orthopraxy." In other words, the implications of*
*the introduction are that a classic apologia—"There have*
*been immoral popes, but they have never said anything against*
*the orthodoxy of the faith"—should now fall into disuse. The*
*apologia would become obsolete because the pope's actions*

*now are to coincide with the orthodoxy of his words. The
starting point of the pontifical magisterium has become its own
example, its own service, and its submission to the same norm
of ethics and charity as binds the other bishops:*

**[30]**   It behooves the Roman Pontiff, as "good and faithful
servant placed by the Lord over his household," to conduct himself in the eyes of the entire church in such wise that he please
the Lord and appear as a righteous model . . . and that the other
bishops and the faithful learn from his example . . . to despise
what is false in this world and extricate themselves from family
and national bonds [*carnis et sanguinis*]. . . .

Wherefore we have proposed, from the very outset of our
pontificate, to submit ourselves, and we do now so submit ourselves, to the same discipline that is incumbent upon the bishops. . . . And although we hope that such popes will succeed us
as will perfume the entire church with the good odor of the
Spirit, nevertheless we wish to indicate to others what we do not
permit ourselves, and we decree . . . [*Bullarium Romanum*,
20:441].

*The wholesome freedom of speech and criticism that had pre-
vailed during the Middle Ages will disappear in the church of
the nineteenth century. The church will not yet have recovered
from the shock occasioned by the bloodletting of the Reform.
It will be terrified by the humiliations to which Napoleon has
subjected it. It will be disconcerted before the apparition of
the modern world, which it will not understand and in which
it will only be able to see the wickedness of Satan, instead of
simply acknowledging the original human ambiguity which
ever corrupts all its own most sacred projects. And so on. Such
a church does not have the wherewithal to permit free speech.
If, in addition to all this, the church finds itself besieged by
pressures and blackmail from the side of the inimical political
interests of the various chancelleries of nineteenth-century Europe, it will be still more hesitant to countenance any extensive
liberty of expression. Indeed, the image of the church — on the
point we are examining — will change radically by comparison
with what we have seen, and for the worse, in the sense that*

*the new attitude will redound to the long-range detriment of the church. Again and again the nineteenth century will see episodes like the Curci affair, in which the founder of* Civiltà Cattolica, *after many years in the directorship of that newspaper, wrote a volume attacking the "real" Vatican, calling for indispensable reforms. But this is the nineteenth century, and Curci only managed to get his work placed on the Index of Forbidden Books.*

*This lack of freedom will be all the more harmful inasmuch as, beginning with the Enlightenment, criticism of the church will now no longer come simply from saints or other loyal persons of the church. Now it will come from outside the church, and be voiced by the so-called freethinkers, the unbelievers of the age.*

*The church will of course be under the objective obligation of responding to these criticisms by reforming and correcting whatever stands in need of reform or correction. True, such criticisms might often be the fruit of hatred. They might be forthcoming by way of an excuse for the will not to believe. But often enough as well, they will express a sincere difficulty, and innocent doubts of faith. When, apropos of the Vatican administration, the chancelleries of Europe begin to observe that the papacy is the "shame of Europe,"[21] it would seem obvious that the pope's duty is not to enhance his power, but to remedy his shame.[22]*

*Perhaps the most notorious of the episodes of the Curci-type was the storm aroused by the publication of Rosmini's book* The Five Wounds of the Church. *Rosmini had completed his work by 1832, but did not dare to publish it until the accession of Pius IX, which seemed to augur a more liberal atmosphere. Today, far from occasioning a sensation, or being regarded as outrageously "progressive," Rosmini's book would be called too theocratic. The author's passion for freedom in the church, however, is unmistakable — an enviable obsession, as we have seen, in the nineteenth century. And Rosmini, too, was placed on the Index. He commented in his diary: "All this work [of investigation against me] was kept from me completely. Nor have I ever been given any reason for the*

*prohibition. I have indicated my total submission.* Sit nomen
Domini benedictum."
    *Following are Rosmini's "five wounds of the church."*
    *1. A division between the people and the clergy in the matter
of public worship (an allusion to the whole problem of Latin
in the liturgy).*
    *2. An inadequate clerical formation (alluding to the scho-
lasticism of the early nineteenth century, which had come to
replace a knowledge of the fathers, whom Rosmini knew so
well).*
    *3. Disunion among the bishops.*
    *4. The appointment of bishops by the secular power, with
severe repercussions where the previous point was concerned.
Rosmini regarded the practice, especially at the hands of Napoleon's France or Josephine's Austria, as a brutal one. Both
powers defended themselves by striving to have Rosmini's book
condemned, availing themselves to this end of every honest
and underhanded means at their disposal. The Austrian ambassador to the Vatican State wrote in a letter that Rosmini
was "our most formidable enemy."*
    *5. The enslavement of the church to material goods. The
following citation from* The Five Wounds of the Church
*develops this last point:*

[31]   The primitive Church was poor, but she was free. Persecution did not rob her of her liberty, as she could not fear to
be robbed of her possessions. She enjoyed neither vassalship nor
protection—still less, patronage, or advocates in her defense.
For it was under these treacherous names that the Church became enslaved to ecclesiastical property. Today it has become
impossible for the Church to maintain her original moral principles relative to the acquisition, governance, and use of material
goods. The Church finds herself in a perilous state, owing to her
forgetfulness of those moral principles of hers which used to
divest earthly goods of their flattering, corrupting force [Ros-
mini, *Quinque Plagae Ecclesiae*, reedition of Clemente Riva
(Brescia: Morcelliana, 1967), p. 320 (no. 20)].

    *Nineteenth-century obstacles to the public expression of opin-
ion in the church did not, however, prevent the existence of*

*that opinion. Had it been at liberty to express itself, public opinion might well have been of great help in the difficult situations in which the church found itself throughout the course of the century. The solution eventually found to the problem of the papal states — later lauded by some popes as a blessing for the church — had long been suggested by not a few critics in the church. If they spoke aloud, however, they were immediately hushed up by Pius IX. The same sort of stifling of expression occurred on lower levels, as well, especially when it could be done in the pope's behalf. When, for example, J. I. Döllinger, still a member of the church, denied that there was anything either "dogmatic," or even, perhaps, "historically necessary," in the temporal power of the pope, he was labeled a "Judas" by the Bishop of Luxembourg. The situation was such that critical opinion could be expressed only at private levels. As one example among many, let us select the letter addressed to Montalembert in March 1859 by Father Meignan, who would one day become Archbishop of Tours and a cardinal:*

[32]   I believe that current conditions have serious disadvantages for religion. We hear that they assure the spiritual independence of the pope. I must deny this categorically. The pope seems still dependent enough to me; and I imagine that God could grant him more independence than that of a priest constantly surrounded by the bayonets of a foreign power, which he must tolerate if he hopes to defend himself against the populations under his obedience. When he was in Rome in 1846, Gregory XVI alternately blessed his subjects and shot them. Pius IX imprisoned them. All of this is necessary to maintain the pope in Rome. And these necessities are hard. I pray that Providence will put an end to a scandal that, if it lasts much longer, will bring about the downfall of Catholicism in Europe and elsewhere [as cited in Daniel-Rops, *La Iglesia de las revoluciones*, 1:434].

*Others — a good many others — thought along similar lines. For example, there was Don Pappalettere, Abbot of Monte Cassino. But there were no opportunities to manifest these atti-*

*tudes. The popes were too skittish politically not to believe that it would be more effective to keep Catholics on a tight leash as a defensive measure against the incursions of the world. And the consequences of this situation were "pathological" manifestations of a too severely repressed opinion. Anonymous pamphlets (one of them the work of ex-Jesuit Passaglia, who in 1854 had actually been a member of the commission that had drafted the bull on the Immaculate Conception), or lurid particulars like the fact that one of the conspirators who in 1853 plotted to assassinate the Pope was a priest, are some of the examples of these "pathological" manifestations of opinion.*

*In the second quarter of the twentieth century, however, this state of affairs began to change. A bitter feeling, experienced by many within the church, had become too strong to ignore—a feeling that Yves M.-J. Congar would one day assert to "have been crystallizing among us for a long time." Congar describes it as arising from a perception of the "inconsistency between what was expected of the Church (namely, the gospel) and what was concretely to be found when one examined this same Church." The sentiment in question had eventually given rise to an entire movement of renewal and reform, which— again according to Congar— "proceeded much more from the purity of the Church than from its impurity." It would not be an exaggeration to assert that this movement of opinion, while it caused so much pain in forcing its way into the church, is responsible for the fact of the Second Vatican Council—one of the hours of history in which human beings have regarded the church as closer to and more like the gospel. Of this broad movement we shall select only a few examples, citing them in chronological order.*

*The first was published in 1946, and is from the pen of a woman. It is called "Letter on the Church" and is presented as a reply to remarks that had been made by a certain nonbeliever who had nostalgically praised the church for so many of the things that insecure nonbelievers sometimes expect from it: a sense of order and security, a solemn, aesthetically appealing liturgy that performs the social function of enabling its participants to escape from life's conflicts, and so on. The*

*author of the "Letter" replies that the church is believed in*
*because it possesses the truth that gives meaning to our lives —*
*not for these aesthetic or tranquilizing gratifications. And she*
*counterbalances the praises of the unbeliever with some criti-*
*cism:*

[33]   An outsider will have difficulty imagining the hunger of
the children of the household in the midst of these overflowing
storehouses of treasures vegetating in granaries.... Do you
imagine that our preachers make any use of the sole genuine
opportunity they have, that of bestowing a bit of the bread of
life on all this well-disposed public, all these poor, teeming
masses of Christians hungering to hear something with a real,
immediate bearing on *their* needs and *their* problems? You would
be utterly dismayed if you had any idea of the idle prattle, di-
vorced from life and empty of both substance and weight, so
often offered us....

And ask employees or teachers who have worked in religious
institutions what they have experienced there by way of social
commitment, or even basic justice in business dealings.... [It
is] as if the "spiritual" life and the "practical" life were two
spheres as far removed from each other as heaven and earth,
without the one being in any way reflected in the other! Why
such vigilance, why such zeal for the defense of powerful ecclesiastical positions, and so little for the growth of the Reign of
God in souls? Why such diffidence and jealousy regarding the
autonomy and initiative of the laity—with all the talk about
"Catholic action" and the "lay apostolate"? ...

The vast coalition of the church with the "conservatives"—
those who actually maintain and are responsible for the states—
may not be an "essential mark" of the church, but it certainly
is a historical fact ... and it is this that has spawned the intimate
involvement of the church with reactionary circles that we so
frequently hear imputed to religion as an essential trait....

None of our criticism is anything but the lament, the angry
lament, of love. Our love refuses to be adolescent love, puppy
love. ("Love is blind.") But it does not fear the chasm its lu-
minous gaze reveals between its ideal for the beloved object and
that object as it is in reality. No, our love is determined to be

serene, wide-eyed, and lucid—to permit itself to examine all reality with unflinching regard, to see things as they are, without illusions, without escape mechanisms, and without excuses, precisely *because* our love expects all things, believes all things, bears all things, and overcomes all things. . . . Would it not be easier to concede nothing and justify everything—which to so many appears as the essence of loyalty to the church? But how does this attitude essentially differ from the "collective vanity" and self-justification that one may be tempted to feel with regard to one's own race or nation—in other words, from a self-complacency so pure as to eliminate from the ego anything but the conviction that one appears exemplary and irreproachable to all one's allies of the same heart? [Ida Görres, "Brief über die Kirche," *Frankfurter Hefte* 1 (1946):719–30].

*At almost the same time that Ida Görres had lifted her voice, another layperson placed his own critical pen at the service of the church. Giovanni Papini's* The Letters of Pope Celestine VI to All Mankind, *which likewise appeared in 1946, eventually found a wide audience. At first the book met with rejection. But then it received a favorable review in* La Civiltà Cattolica *(December 1946, pp. 369–76), where one could read Papini's own words to the effect that his "letters" had sprung directly from an abyss of sorrow and despair (World War II had just ended), but in the faith and the hope that the message of Christ could be in time to rescue humankind from the maelstrom into which it had been swept. The figure of Celestine VI took shape in Papini's fantasy as a product of this contrast "of most vivid pain and inexhaustible love, of desperation and hope" (p. 370). The author introduces his work with two particularly pregnant texts from the Gospels: "The last shall be first" (Matt. 20:16); and "Were these to keep silent, the very stones would cry out" (Luke 19:40). Both seem to refer to the author's condition as a layperson in the church of Pius XII.*

*It is the first four letters that are important for our purposes. These are addressed respectively to the people, to priests, to religious, and to theologians. The first letter, to the whole peo-*

*ple of God, the one true church, is entitled "To the People Who Call Themselves Christian."*

[34]  We live too comfortably and complacently behind the stone walls of our church. We too readily believe, through ignorance or sloth, that it is enough to attend Mass, to follow the sacred Liturgy, to make an act of penitence every once in a while, to put a penny in a beggar's palm, to respect, through fear of imprisonment or fear of hell, three or four Commandments. . . .

In order to defend itself against secular power, to protect itself against the arrogant obstinacy of heretics, to maintain discipline among its subjects, to sustain its almost imperial sovereignty, [the Roman church] has retarded its true impulse, it has mixed politics with its completely spiritual mission, and seems often reduced to a community administrative government, merely supplying the Sacraments and diligently maintaining an enormous office crowded with clerks.

The Church has become transformed, a little because of its assailants, a little because of its own guardians, into a doctrinal, disciplinary, and liturgical fortress. . . . God intended it to be a pyre on a mountain top, and we have scattered it, that divine flame, in so many tiny candles that smoke and sputter at the end of solemn, ancient naves, where many do not go. . . .

Too often the Pontiffs, instead of being Vicars of God, eternally inspired and inspiring, were merely continuations of that too human Peter who wished to erect a tent on the Mount of Transfiguration, not of the Peter impetuous and generous who first recognized in the homeless prophet the Son of God, but of that Peter who needed the look of the captured and the song of the cock to discover himself, of that Peter who would not keep vigil that last night in the Garden of Olives and who raised an ineffectual sword against a minor actor in the drama of Redemption [Giovanni Papini, *The Letters of Pope Celestine VI to All Mankind* (New York: E. P. Dutton and Co., Inc., 1948), pp. 22, 24–25, 27].

*The second letter is addressed to priests. Papini is harsh. He will be even more severe with religious, as we shall see below.*

*But priests, too, hold a Treasure in their hands that ought to*
*have seared away their mediocrity.*

[35]   Christ called you "the salt of the earth." Why, then, is
the world still so insipid, so stupid; insipid almost to the point
of vapidity, stupid to the point of imbecility? If the present
wretchedness of mankind is a result of abandonment of Christianity, of the non-Christianity of Christians, of the non-conver-
sion of Christians, who, more than you, ought to assume the
major burden of blame? And I cannot refrain from asking you:
Do you truly believe in God? Do you really know Christ? . . .

Too many of you seem but simple clerks of the Church—
ushers, beadles, writers, and bookkeepers—instead of apostles,
sleepless, impatient, and imperious. Too many of you are som-
nolent and mechanical administrators of the sacraments instead
of witnesses, confessors, and radiant examples of the truth which
gushed forth from the lips of the Redeemer. You should be as
living trees on the heights, refuges for the birds of the air, generous as leaves, flowers, fruit, and shade; and instead you are,
more often than not, merely bare, smooth stakes, at times well
varnished, but with no roots in the humus of humanity, giving
forth neither buds nor blossoms; inferior wood, dead wood fit
only to construct fences and barriers, to carry manifestoes of
prohibition and regulation. . . .

I suffer, not because of your corruption, but because of your
mediocrity. Your life today is much purer than in other centuries. One could not write of you a "Book of Gomorrah," as did
St. Peter Damian. The userers, the fornicators, the sodomists,
the simonists, the arch heretics, have almost disappeared among
you. Indeed, during my long journey, I recall having met young
priests in whom the will to serve Christ shone luminously in a
pallor of love, like a living flame behind an alabaster lamp. I
recall having known aged priests venerated more for the light
of their charity than for the whiteness of their locks; who were
consumed in God, as the anonymous, glittering candle of the
poor dissolves before the Most Holy. But I have also seen priests
more impassioned by money or hunting than by their ministry,
more eager for a good cook than a good name; more avid for
politics or possessions than for watching over the salvation of

their flocks, more expert in gossiping than in edifying. Many of them seemed, rather than like priests of Christ, like well-fed stewards, country squires, diligent solicitors of worldly affairs, narrow-minded bourgeois merchants who merely by chance happened to go into the spiritual life.

And of course there are also among you doctors, scholars, savants, pedants, those who know how to compose a sonnet for the bishop, who can draft the little speech for the First Communion, prepare the little manual of spiritual exercises, the monograph on the calendar of the diocese, the "scientific" tract crammed with "sound" principles, pregnant with "solid" doctrine. Some of you can preach sermons more flowery than the rectory garden; homilies more rich in unction than an olive-press, sermons more assiduously harmonious than a harmonium. At times from the pulpit you dispense orations so knowing with persuasive harmony of voice that your own ears listen to your lips with a delight not only ineffable but apparent.

But rarely do your words burst from the heart to shoot straight at other hearts, to touch and overturn them. They have the smell of oil rather than the odor of the sun. But today, to twist and wring the spirit, we need the freshness of love and simplicity rather than the intricacies and trappings of pleading eloquence. . . .

But do you not think perhaps that your coldness alienates the eager souls, that your poverty of heart repels the generous spirits, that your measured mediocrity is repugnant to the spirit thirsty for the sublime, that the insularity of your too cautious minds discourages the free souls? . . .

Put aside, for the time being, the innumerable devotions to which the still half-pagan masses of people are so addicted, the devotions which you tolerate with such condescension and yet stimulate and cultivate. No one more than I venerates the Virgin Mother, the queenly servant of the King of Kings, who is above all women. But do not act so that it appears to the profane and spiteful that Catholicism, even if only among the devotion of the common people, is a cult of the Madonna more than of the Trinity. You remember the Father but a little; still less the Holy Ghost. If it were not for the "Our Father" and the "Creed," the Creator of heaven and earth, the Consoler who baptized the

Apostles with fire, would be much less remembered by you than are Mary and the Saints [Papini, *Letters*, pp. 32, 34, 36–37, 38–39].

*Perhaps the third letter, "To the Monks and Brothers," merits the closest attention, since it can be said that some of Papini's criticisms presage many of the traits that have characterized religious life since Vatican II.*

**[36]** Those brothers who should have mixed with people to fight heresy and bring to the people the living and speaking example of the Gospel, shut themselves up in their monasteries, where, notwithstanding their professed poverty, they lack none of the most common needs of life, and go out only to celebrate a few Masses, preach a few sermons, to assist some parish priest, and give a few instructions according to a proscribed curriculum in an accredited and qualified school.

They should have been like indefatigable gulls, wheeling in the open air, screaming and scolding along every shore; among the weary, the laborers, the beggars, and the lost; and instead they are like birds who no longer fly, but are content to rustle among papers and scratch among the library books, to cluck in the church choir and peck in the refectory. . . .

You do not mix enough in the melting pot of life. You do not seek enough the company of men, even though they be evildoers or rogues. You do not run enough to help souls in danger, going even where you are not called, to share with your torment in the tortures of your brothers. . . . You are too segregated in your convents, too retired in your sanctuaries, too muffled up in your cells. . . . Certain Orders are nothing more than machines devoted solely to the internal production of brothers of that same Order. . . .

In the name of God and of man, leave your learned texts at times, and your peaceful cloisters, roll up your sleeves, grasp that cross that has the form of a sword and go out in the fields to give a helping hand to the men of good will who work so that on this earth, after so much desolation, may be founded the kingdom of heaven. . . .

He who lives in prayer and renunciation to achieve his own

salvation is not yet a saint. He is the purest of the egoists, but in the eyes of the abandoned he is always the one who thinks only of his own soul and his own salvation. Today the world is strewn with mountains of ashes; it is a limitless hospital, an immense lunatic asylum. You cannot remain tranquil in your basilicas, in your scholastic halls, your libraries, your cells. God calls you with a great voice, with all the ringing power of His infinite love, to save His people. . . .

In this hour of imminent barbarity, charity is the paramount necessity. . . . For you and for all, the day of the supreme test has arrived. Either man chooses to practice Christianity daily and joyfully, even if it be in its most elementary precepts, or he will be condemned to the most horrible agony, to the tortures of an earthly hell which will end only in universal slaughter and universal suicide. Priests, monks, brothers, yours is the chief role in this gigantic work of conversion. . . .

It will be a wonderful day for humanity when you leave your cloisters to journey over the highways of the world.

. . . Perhaps the Holy Ghost, as in other epochs, will arouse a predestined one to found a new Order, an Order more suited to the needs of the times, an Order that will not close its followers in the dull shadows of its convent, but will urge them to be as men among men [Papini, *Letters*, pp. 45, 46–47, 49, 50–51, 51–52].

*And finally, the letter to the theologians, too, denounces certain unseemly elements of which later theology will divest itself:*

[37] Why, then, is divine Theology so unpopular among men today? Why is the supreme science, the science of God, ignored today even among the educated? Why do we see it, above all in our own Church, relegated to seminary classrooms and monastery lecture halls? Why do those times seem fabulous, those times when bakers and drapers as well as men of the world and men of letters argued passionately in the markets and salons on the problems of Incarnation and Grace? . . . Does a doubt never present itself to your minds that the maximum blame for such a lamentable desertion may be yours? . . .

The truth, the sad truth, is that fiery, creative thought has passed from you. . . . Only the great heresies succeeded for a time in inflaming the spirits and in stirring the minds. The initiative has passed from you to your enemies, the philosophers; and today, we can say, there is no well-informed, educated lay person who either heeds your work or is enthusiastic over your opinions. . . . For hundreds of years you have trodden and retrodden the highway of tradition and left it in such a dark and impassable condition that even the most intrepid travelers prefer to clamber up the paths of a rocky mountain, or lose themselves in the undergrowth of a forest. . . .

For centuries, you theologians have been little more than compilers of synopses, manipulators of manuals, registrars of the commonplace, nothing more than tedious commentators, exhumers, annotators, and rearrangers of ancient, hoary texts. To be sure, a just, diligent, well-documented repetition, but nevertheless repetition. Has it never occurred to you that warmed-over foods, in the long run, become a bore even to the greedy; that foods cooked and recooked in the same old pots, with the same old sauces, end by disgusting even the most patient palates? . . .

It is not true that all has been said, and that we are nothing but the speaking trumpets of the dead. Every century the journey of the spirit begins anew. . . . Go out at times into the open air, listen to the voices of those who are hungry for truth, do not scorn to learn something from the nontheologians. I tell you to listen first to the poets. You will be great theologians if you do not overlook some poetic quality. . . . St. Augustine the theologian was a poet, even as Dante the poet was a theologian. But you are horrified before the ardor, the beauty, the music of thought. . . . You theorize on the human mind, and yet you do not perceive that near you are eager, enthusiastic minds, which perhaps await only one word from you to precede you upon the stairs that climb to eternity. . . . The study of God is so stupendous that it seems to me a sign of pride in you not to seek and accept all human collaboration—even that of the divine children who are the poets, of those children whom Jesus called to Himself—pre-figurations of poets who are, if inferior to saints, immeasurably superior to those who philosophize. . . . My predecessors have cautioned you to prudence, because many of you were, at one time, too daring. Today, because you are floundering and gasping in a sea of indifference and monotony, I exhort you to daring exploits [Papini, *Letters*, pp. 55, 56–57, 59–60, 61].

●

*As I shall remark in the course of the last part of this anthology, it is the sins of the system, rather than personal sins, that are criticized in modern writings on the church. This is quite clear. It is not particular behavior that is denounced, but procedures. The criticism is institutional, then, rather than personal. For example, we have this important passage from Congar:*

[38]   [W. Foerster] shows how a certain approach to recruiting personnel for the central administration actually ends up "not reinforcing papal power, but simply isolating it." If such administrators were to be selected only from among persons of a certain type, persons with a certain mentality—for example, if they were to be of a generally conservative, tutiorist mindset, and see in tradition, and fidelity to that tradition, scarcely anything but the static aspect, persons who are likely to pose the fewest problems, spring the fewest surprises, and embark on no adventures—obviously what we should have between the central power and the periphery would be an instrument of isolation, a "party," as it were. Doubtless this sort of instrument would respond to certain demands, like security, or moderation. But it would leave other, equally sacred demands—those of a body everlastingly restless for conquest, adaptation, and progress— without response. A number of the thoughts or aspirations at work in the church, especially in the dynamic elements of the church, could never really be heard.

The problem is serious enough that one feels allowed—because one feels obligated—to pose it, very respectfully, but frankly [Yves M.-J. Congar, *Vraie et fausse réforme dans l'église* (Paris: Cerf, 1968), pp. 275–76].

*A disapproval of institutional procedures, rather than of personal behavior, is likewise reflected in the following text from*

*Karl Rahner. The author is engaging in a personal lament,
really, rather than in any formal criticism, and he couches his
reflection in an account of certain personal experiences. But
although it is a personal lament, because he voices it many
years after those personal experiences had occurred, it can no
longer be misinterpreted as serving the purpose of some personal vendetta. Rahner's only interest is the reform of certain
behavior of the official church. I include it in this anthology
because, while it was published only in 1975, the events it
relates occurred before the Second Vatican Council (our
chronological terminus). It appeared in the periodical* Orientierung *under the eloquent title "Erlebtes" ("What I have
experienced in my life"), and was presented by the author in
support of a series of proposals for church reform being made
by the periodical.*

[39]   In pre-Vatican-II days I received from Rome, through my
Father General, an order forbidding me to do any public speaking, at the instigation of a German bishop now deceased. Again
through my Father General I received from Rome an order
prohibiting me from publishing anything on the subject of the
concelebration of the Eucharist. Likewise through my Father
General Rome imposed on me the obligation of submitting to
Roman censorship everything I might write. With the Council
over, all of this belongs to the past, and of itself holds no current
interest. Its historical interest lies in the fact that all of these
measures proceeded from the Holy Office, and yet it was the
Father General of my order who was obliged to communicate
them to me. Neither the Holy Office nor my Father General
ever gave me written justification for these measures, not even
in the form of an anonymous judgment. In private conversation,
the then Father General, a person of impeccable orthodoxy and
strict loyalty to the Holy Office, confessed to me, "You see,
Father, I never know when, or whom, or how, their thunderbolts
are going to strike."

During the Council, Cardinal Ottaviani himself admitted to
me that all of these measures had indeed issued from the Holy
Office. And yet he never communicated to me, either in writing
or in express words, their withdrawal. As we see, it was not the

practice of the Rome of that time to extend such delicate courtesy to a lowly religious.

A great many things have improved since those days. However, it seems to me, not everything is yet as it should be. Superiors General of religious orders continue all too frequently to be obliged to act simply as the letter carriers of Roman organisms, and nevertheless to convey the communication in question as if they had taken such and such particular measures on their own initiative. Furthermore, it seems to me, despite their obligation to obey, these Generals also have the right, depending on the case, to tell Rome that their conscience prevents them from adopting certain measures as their own, and to ask the Roman superior to show his face and be the one to contact the person involved [Karl Rahner, "Erlebtes," *Orientierung*, January 15, 1975, p. 4].

*I have remarked that Rahner never made his criticism of the church a matter of personal retaliation. In an interview granted to* Vida Nueva *on the occasion of his eightieth birthday, he was asked whether there was anything he regretted over the course of his long life. One of the things he regretted, he said, is that he had not had more courage vis-à-vis those who have authority in the church* (Vida Nueva, *March 24, 1984, p. 29). For this reason, and because this anthology is being composed in the very year of the great theologian's death, I shall present a second text from Rahner. Following is a statement he made during the time of the council. Its words may seem hard, but its context, which there is no room to discuss here, establishes their intent: to help correct the harm done the credibility of the church not only by its faults, but by the failure of persons of the church to acknowledge these faults. Rahner acknowledges that many people feel this way today.*

[40]   There stands the Church, and she declares herself necessary for salvation, she comes to us in the name of a holy God, she declares herself to be in possession of all truth and grace, she claims to be the one ark of salvation among the flood of sin and corruption, she believes herself commissioned to convert

and save all men. And this very Church which comes to us with such claims, why, look at her! — so they will say — look how she seems to use two different yardsticks: *she proclaims to poor, troubled humanity the Sermon on the Mount with its "impossible" demands, but her official representatives seem to let these demands rest very lightly on their own personal shoulders.* Don't they all seem to live pretty comfortable lives? Aren't they often avaricious or arrogant or overbearing? Isn't there a continuous succession of scandals, even in the ranks of her religious orders, who after all are supposed to be striving for holiness and perfection? Are the bad popes a mere catch-phrase or aren't they a historical fact? And haven't even her holiest things been continually misused in all sorts of ways for sinful purposes: the confession and the sacraments in general, the papacy used for transparently political purposes, and so on? [Karl Rahner, *Theological Investigations*, vol. 6 (New York: Crossroad, 1982), p. 254; emphasis added].

> *Finally, let us conclude this series of examples with a solemn, very well-known passage, once more from the pen of Karl Rahner, which further develops this characteristic element of modern criticism of the church: criticism as a defense precisely of the credibility of the church. That credibility is recognized to be jeopardized in the eyes of the world through attitudes and procedures too little in keeping with the spirit of the gospel. The following reading is taken from a talk first given in Barcelona in 1962 "on the possibility of faith today." The church itself, the author says, is actually one of the three great obstacles to faith for men and women of the twentieth century.*

[41] There is, however, a further hindrance and danger to faith besides the deep bitterness of human existence and the great variety of philosophies of life in the world. I am referring to the assembly of believers itself — the Church. She is indeed the holy Church, even in the view of any unprejudiced student of history. She is the sign which, lifted up above all nations, bears her own testimony to her divine origin and life by her inexhaustible fruitfulness for all holiness. But she is also the sinful Church of sinners, the sinful Church, because we her members are sinners.

And this sinfulness of the Church does not merely mean the sum total of the, as it were, private faults and failures of her members, including even those who bear her highest and most sacred offices. The sinfulness and inadequacy of the members of the Church have their effects also in the actions and conduct which, insofar as they take place within the sphere of human experience, must be designated as the actions and conduct of the Church herself. Sinful human nature, insufficiency, finiteness, shortsightedness, a falling short of the demands of the times, lack of understanding for the needs of the times, for her duties and for the trends of the future — all these most human characteristics also belong both to the office-bearers and to all the members of the Church and they also take effect by God's permissive will in what the Church is and does. It would be silly self-deceit and clerical pride, group-egoism and cult of personality as found in totalitarian systems — which does not become the Church as the congregation of Jesus, the meek and humble of Heart — if it were to deny all this, or tried to hush it up or to minimize it, or made out that this burden was merely the burden of the Church of previous ages which has now been taken from her. No, the Church is the Church of poor sinners; she is the Church which does not have the courage to regard the future as belonging to God in the same way as she has experienced the past as belonging to God. She is often in the position of one who glorifies her past and looks askance at the present, insofar as she has not created it herself, finding it all too easy to condemn it. She is often the one who, in questions of science, does not only proceed slowly and carefully — intent on preserving the purity of the Faith — but also often waits too long and who, in the nineteenth and twentieth century has sometimes been too quick to say "no" when she could have pronounced a "yes" earlier than she did — with, of course, the necessary nuances and distinctions. She has quite often in the past sided more with the powerful and made herself too little the advocate of the poor. Often she has not proclaimed her criticisms of the powerful of this world loudly enough, so that it looked as if she were trying to procure an alibi for herself without really coming into conflict with the great ones of this world. She often places more value on the bureaucratic apparatus of the Church than in the enthusiasm of her Spirit; she often loves the calm more than the storm, the old (which has proved itself) more than the new (which is bold and daring). Often in the past, she has in her office-bearers wronged saints, thinkers, those who were painfully looking for an answer, and theologians — all of whom wanted merely to give her their selfless service. Often before she has warded off public opinion in the Church, although according to Pius XII such public opinion is essential to the well-being of the Church. Not infrequently she has mistaken the barren mediocrity of an average theology and philosophy for the clarity of a good scholastic tradition. She has often shown herself more in the role of an anathematizing judge to those outside her fold, to the Orthodox and Protestants, than in the form of a loving mother who meets her child half-way — as far as she can possibly go — in all humility and without being controversial. She has frequently failed to recognize the spirit which is really her own when, as is its way, it has breathed where it would through the alleys of the history of the world and not merely through the sacred halls of the Church herself. Often before, she has let herself be pulled down by heresies and other movements — contrary to her proper nature and the fullness of her truth (although without ever denying that truth) — to the level of onesidedness of her opponents. And often in such cases she has represented her teaching, not as the more comprehensive "yes" to what was the "proper" and latent meaning of the heresy, but rather as what appeared to be a purely dialectic "no" given to such a heresy. According to every human estimation she has missed many a golden opportunity in the achievement of her task, or has wanted to seize it when the kairos for it was already past. Not infrequently, while being under the impression that she was championing the lofty inexorability of the divine law (which is certainly her sacred duty), she was really acting like a common, nagging governess, trying narrow-mindedly and with too average an understanding of human existence to regulate life by the typical "Examination of Conscience" (*Beichtspiegel*) still found in devotional prayer-books which might have been suitable for the famous "Lieschen Müller"[23] in the even tenor of the provincial town of the nineteenth century. She has too often asked merely for well-ordered good breeding which never puts a foot wrong, instead of asking for a mind with high ideals, a loving heart and courageous life. To many minds she has not been able to give an authentic enough account of herself for people to see guilt and dark fate existing only outside her [Rahner, *Theological Investigations*, vol. 5, pp. 15–17].

# PART II

# THE REASONS

I Am Not Ashamed of the Gospel. Woe To Me If I Do Not Preach It! (Rom. 1:16; 1 Cor. 9:16)

The Spirit Breathes Where It Will...for God Has Chosen the Weak To Confound the Mighty (John 3:8; 1 Cor. 1:27)

# TEXTS WITH COMMENTARY

## ECCLESIAL ASPECTS

<small>THE STONE WITH WHICH WE STRIKE OUR BREAST IS
THE ONE THAT OUR ENEMIES HAVE NOT CAST AT US</small>
[Giovanni Papini, *The Letters of Pope Celestine VI*].

*Before ever entertaining any express reflection on the foun-*
*dation and conditions of criticism, the saints personally lived*
*this foundation and these conditions in their actual praxis.*
*We, too, can take this praxis as the point of departure of our*
*quest for a more explicit reflection. Around the year 600, the*
*great Irish monk St. Columban, Abbot of Luxeuil, persecuted*
*by Queen Brunhilde for reasons very akin to the motive for*
*the beheading of John the Baptist, wrote a letter to Pope Bon-*
*iface IV complaining of a number problems of church unity*
*in pastoral and dogmatic matters. In the interest of impartiality*
*I might add that St. Columban himself did not always con-*
*tribute a great deal to this unity, with his insistence that certain*
*Irish customs be observed throughout Europe (including, in-*
*cidentally, the use of secret confession in the Sacrament of*
*Reconciliation). But the prologue of Columban's letter to Bon-*
*iface deserves to be cited here because of the attitude it reflects.*

[42]    To the Supreme Head of all the churches of Europe . . . to
the Highest from the lowest . . . to the First from the last . . . to
a mighty one from (will wonders never cease?) someone weak
and lowly:

Who will hear me? Who will not at once demand to see this
presumptuous charlatan who dares write all of this without being
asked? Who will not tell me what Moses heard from the lips of
the Hebrew who was abusing his brother: "Who has appointed
you judge over me?" (Exod. 2:14)?

But I shall reply: there is no such thing as overdoing a response to the *need for the upbuilding of the church*. And if perchance I seem to you to be a person of little account, then attend not to who it is who writes, but to what it is that is written. For why should a Christian pilgrim refrain from mentioning what goes without saying in the minds of his Arian neighbors? Surely there could be no reason for silence in such circumstances. After all, wounds inflicted by a friend are less harmful than the deceitful kisses of an enemy (Prov. 27:6)! Others gleefully whisper in secret; I shall speak out publicly, in pain and affliction. . . . For it is not vanity or temerity that moves this unimportant person to address men of such lofty estate. It is sorrow, and not pomposity, that impels me to say that, in you who contend with one another, "the name of God is blasphemed among the nations" (Rom. 1:22) [St. Columban, *Epistolae ad Diversos*, 5 (*PL* 80:274–75)].

> *In Part 1, in examining an excerpt from a letter of St. Catherine of Siena, we observed Catherine's existential reason for speaking out, even were she thereby to seem to contradict her doctrinal content. St. Jerome expresses the same motive, couching it in theoretical terms: if and when the church sins, if that sin happens to be committed by a higher authority, then by this very fact it is a far more serious sin, and it must not be allowed to continue. Jerome writes as follows:*

[43]   Samaria and Sodom—that is, the heretics and the gentiles—frequently sin less seriously than they who hold themselves forth as Jerusalem—that is, than the men of the church. So it was that the Corinthians, who of course believed in Christ, were reproached by St. Paul for their wicked deeds: "There is such impurity among you as does not exist even among the gentiles" (1 Cor. 5:11). . . . And while Sodom and Samaria are evil, they are not half so sinful as Jerusalem! "For the servant who knows the will of his master and does not do it, will receive many stripes" (Luke 12:47). . . . Who will doubt, then, that, among three sinners, or even criminals—one a gentile, the second a heretic, and the third an ecclesiastic—the one whose dignity is loftiest will deserve a far more severe punishment? . . . The least, meanwhile, will win mercy. . . . Nor

does St. Peter speak differently: "The time has come for judgment to begin with the house of God" (1 Pet. 4:17). And the prophet upon whom we are making this commentary says to those who come armed with battle-axes, "Begin at my sanctuary" (Ezek. 9:6). . . . We read the same in the Gospel: "On the day of judgment the land of Sodom will fare better than those cities that refused to receive the apostles" (Matt. 10:15) [St. Jerome, *Commentary on Ezekiel (PL* 25:153, 155, 157)].

*The greater responsibility borne by the higher authority does not spring from personal factors (from someone's having "received more"), but from the "social" purpose of the church. The church exists to serve. Authority is bestowed on persons of the church in view of the duty of the church to make faith possible in the world. The church, as a "sacrament of Christ and of salvation," does not exist for its own sake. It exists for the sake of a composition or synthesis of two pairs of opposita: it exists that the salvation of God may reach human sin, and that the human being's promise may attain to its truth, which is the Word of God. The consideration that faith may fall into danger is a crucial one in the following passage from Thomas Aquinas, since when faith is threatened, no member of the church can feel altogether free of the responsibility to avert the threat.*

[44]  [On the one hand it would seem that] superiors are not to be corrected by their subjects. . . . Moreover, dealing with the text where St. Paul [in Galatians 2] says "I opposed him [Peter] to his face," a gloss adds the words, "as an equal." And so, as a subject is not his superior's equal, he should not correct him.

Besides, Gregory says, "Only he who is conscious of being better himself, should presume to correct the lives of holy men." But a man should not feel that he is better than his superior. Consequently superiors are not to be corrected.

On the other hand is the advice of the *Rule* of Augustine, "Have mercy not only on yourselves but also on him, who, being in a higher position among you, is therefore in greater danger." Now fraternal correction is a work of mercy. Therefore superiors also are to be corrected. . . .

"To oppose anyone to his face in public" goes beyond the due measure of fraternal correction; and for this reason Paul would not have rebuked Peter if he were not in some way his equal as far as the defense of the faith was concerned. . . . Note, however, that where there is real danger to the faith, subjects must rebuke their superiors *even publicly*. On this account Paul, who was subject to Peter, publicly rebuked him when there was imminent danger of scandal in a matter of faith. . . .

It is presumption and pride for a man to think he is better in all points than his superior. But not if he regards himself as better in some particular respect, for in this life there is no one without some defect. Furthermore, remember that when a man charitably reproves a superior it does not mean that he thinks himself any better than him, but merely that he is giving help to someone "who, being in a higher position, is therefore in greater danger," as Augustine remarks in his *Rule* [Thomas Aquinas, *Summa Theologiae* (London: Blackfriars), vol. 34, 2a2ae. 33, 4, 2 and 3].

*This clear, forthright statement of St. Thomas cannot, of course, be regarded as attempting to give an adequate reply to the question of just when the danger of scandal, or of threat to the faith, is present. Perhaps we ought to add that, in a pluralistic society like ours today, in which the church no longer coincides with the citizenry as a whole, and where the whole of the citizenry no longer belongs to the church by birth, this threat and this scandal may be much more frequent than in a society of Christendom. At all events, this teaching of Thomas had a considerable influence on many of the theologians of the Middle Ages, especially in the Dominican order. For example, Juan de Torquemada, in one of the masterpieces of medieval ecclesiology, poses a number of questions (71, 72) concerning the authority of the Roman pontiff. Among them figure the following two: whether the object of fraternal correction includes the pope; and whether it might ever be in order to criticize the pope publicly. And, following Thomas, Torquemada answers in the affirmative in each instance* (Summa de Ecclesia, *Salamanca, 1560, pp. 630–31). Likewise John of Paris, in chapter 22 of his treatise on royal and papal power, writes:*

[45]  In a case where the pope manifestly errs, for example by refusing to respect the rights of the churches, or by scandalizing the church by some type of conduct, he may be judged, reasoned with, and reprehended by anyone at all, if not in virtue of the critic's office, then out of the zeal of charity; and not through the imposition of a punishment, but by way of a reverent exhortation, since any consideration owed anyone is owed more to the pope by reason of the higher condition to which he has been elevated.

In other words, just as the pope, by reason of the state to which he has been elevated, is ... thereby ... bound to correct others in a fraternal and charitable manner—although saving his authority, as Augustine says—so also conversely, ... if the pope has been remiss, then one is no less bound to correct him in a fraternal and charitable manner, preserving all humility and reverence. Wherefore in Galatians, chapter 2, when Peter had come to Antioch, Paul "resisted him to his face," as he was indeed deserving of reprimand. Therefore it is improper to say that one "reaches too high" or "storms heaven" in justly reprimanding a high authority. "Heaven" is cited too lightly in this context, since where the pope manifestly offends, this is not heaven. Nor is he being "stormed" or attacked, since the one correcting him is acting precisely in his behalf.

Nor need one fear lest the pope be scandalized on this account, since passive scandal is to be found not in perfect men, but only in the spiritually immature. Therefore to fear scandal to the pope in this is to hold that the pope is spiritually immature, and less perfect than another whom one ought indeed to correct boldly when delinquent; and therefore they indeed "storm heaven" who thus imply of the Holy Father that he is vindictive and that he takes it ill that his deeds be judged in any way, which certainly is not to be held, since he is not spiritually immature, but perfect, and more perfect than others [John of Paris, *Tractatus de Potestate Regia et Papali*, in Leclerq, ed., *Jean de Paris et l'ecclésiologie du XIII siècle* (Paris, 1942), pp. 249–50].

*The text from Thomas Aquinas, cited above, makes it clear
that criticism in the church may never be utilized for purposes
of a personal power struggle. It must emerge exclusively from
the danger of harm to the gospel, which "burns" the hands of
the one holding it.*

*Another St. Thomas — a "man for all seasons" and the
fashioner of utopias — saw aright here. His name was Thomas
More.*

[46]    Must one then maintain a respectful silence upon all manner of abuses? Is all criticism of the evils begotten of human
wickedness to be dubbed novelty, absurdity, impertinence? Then
let us renounce the name of Christian, for we are to shroud in
silence the teaching of Christ. Almost all the precepts of Jesus
condemn the customs of the day far more than any criticism that
may come forth from my tongue or pen [as cited by E. Der-
mengheim, *Erasme et Thomas More contre Machiavel* (Paris,
1926), p. 235].

*In that passionate paragraph, St. Thomas More is only putting
into practice the recommendations of St. Augustine regarding
a problem for all seasons. It is often argued that telling the
truth can be harmful, because there may be people who are
not ready for it and who will therefore be harmed by it. Thereupon it is the temptation of many minds to have recourse to
a lie in order to do good. In his treatise on perseverance,
Augustine poses just such a problem. In order to get people to
pray more, will it be better to say that God does not know
what we need? After all, if we say, as Jesus did, that God
already knows ahead of time what we are asking for, there
are those who will be less inclined to pray. Here Augustine
pauses to observe that, in our manner of speaking the truth,
it is sometimes possible to couch that truth in such terms as
will make it "milk for babies and solid food for adults" at the
same time. But he also knows that there will be cases in which
it will be too idealistic of us to hope to be able to speak in
this manner. And so he asks: What should we do in more
difficult cases?*

[47]    One must therefore tell the truth, especially when a difficulty makes it all the more urgent that truth be told. Let those grasp it who can. Far be it that, in keeping silence out of consideration for those who might not be able to understand, not only truth be frustrated, but those be left in error who could have grasped the truth and thus escaped their error. . . .

But when the case is such that if we state it as it actually is, those who cannot understand it will become worse persons, what must we do then? Speak the truth, and let those who can, understand. We must not remain silent. For if we do, neither will the capable nor the incapable understand, and now it is the more intelligent who will become worse persons. Conversely, if the more intelligent hear and understand the truth, they will be able to teach it to many of the others. . . . How fearful we are that the truth may harm those who will not be able to understand! Why are we not afraid that if we remain silent, those who could have understood will be deceived! [St. Augustine of Hippo, *De Bono Perseverantiae*, chap. 16 (*PL* 45:1017–18)].

> *Augustine's view has endured down to our day. Precisely because it is the sacrament of salvation for humanity, the church is also, at certain moments, a paradigm of the sin of this humanity. Thus the church comes to be a kind of "concentrate" of all that humanity, in which sin and the Spirit of God, original wickedness and the grace of Christ, are simultaneously at work. This would seem to be the view of Emile Mersch, one of the great ecclesiologists of the Mystical Body of Christ in the twentieth century.*

[48]    Mankind is sinful. It bears the burden of its former crimes, and adds to it by its present crimes. . . . Consequently an intense desire for justice and love, a longing for a better mankind in a better world, is formed and quickened in it, not without the aid of grace. But the longing is so vague . . . and its manifestations are so incoherent, tentative, and divergent, that these divergencies often pass for antagonisms. The steps proposed for reaching agreement evoke challenges, and the latter multiply in the measure that the efforts are more numerous and deficient. Misunderstandings are added to misunderstandings, and a psy-

chosis of insecurity and hostility develops. If certain unfortunate circumstances arise, if some more than ordinarily brutal display of selfishness occurs, disaster results. Men give way to terror and madness and passion, and wrath and carnage flare up; . . . and then we have the tragedy of a blind and raging giant who turns his own weapons against himself and rends himself to pieces in the night.

Such is the humanity that makes up the Church. We are dealing here with a delicate subject that is a source of dismay and scandal. We can readily understand that the Church should have its martyrs and that the innocent may be persecuted or succumb to illness. But that Christ's spouse, whom He has taken to make her holy and spotless, without defilement or blemish of any sort, that Christ's body, which God has chosen from eternity to adorn with the grace of adoption in purity and sanctity, should be a body of sin, that it should be demeaned by pettiness and malice, and that its moral miseries should figure so largely even in its most characteristic activity, seems impossible to concede.

But it is so. The holy mystical body is a body in which redemption is accomplished and yet not accomplished; in which sin is ever present and active [Emile Mersch, *The Theology of the Mystical Body* (St. Louis: Herder, 1951), pp. 306–7].

*At other times it is argued that there is no place for criticism in the church because the church is holy. We are told that the very fact of criticism is a denial of this holiness, so that criticism would in and of itself be an assault on the sanctity and dignity of the church. St. Augustine answers this difficulty by pointing out the eschatological nature of the church's sanctity — which, while already present, nevertheless is "not yet." This same principle will help us understand the true dignity of the church.*

[49]   [Only on the day of judgment] the church will be "without blemish or wrinkle or anything of the kind," for only then will it be genuinely glorious. After all, Scripture not only says: "to present itself a church without blemish or wrinkle," but then goes on to say, "and glorious" (Eph. 5:27). Thereby we are given to understand, altogether clearly, that the church will only be

clean and pure when it is glorious. But surely, amidst the wickedness of our day, amidst such great scandals and the licentious deeds of the perverse, the church can scarcely be said to be glorious by the fact that "kings serve her" — since this is precisely her greatest and most perilous temptation. . . . As mediator, the Lord joined himself to the Church under the form of a Slave, and was not glorified until the day of the Resurrection (cf. John 7:39). This being the case, how are we to say that the Church is glorious even before her resurrection? No, in the interim God is cleansing her, using the water of the Word, and effacing her past sins in order to extirpate from her the empire of the evil angels. Only later will he bring her healing to completion, and cause her to be that glorious figure "without blemish or wrinkle" [Augustine of Hippo, *De Perfectione Iustitiae Hominis*, chap. 15 (*PL* 44:310)].

> *These or similar words appear countless times in St. Augustine as he wrestles with the Donatists and their claim that only the holy and the pure were true members of the church. Accordingly, we must assert that a hierarchy that would refuse to tolerate criticism on grounds of the holiness of the church would be guilty of what we might call a "reverse Donatism."*
>
> *God, meanwhile, with a view to this ongoing purification of a church whose holiness is eschatological, constantly makes use of human means. Surely this is the meaning of the myriad challenges with which the church is endlessly beset. The gospel must never be comfortable, not even for the church. The church is necessarily surrounded by constant challenges. This is one of the clearest lessons of church history. As Yves M.-J. Congar puts it:*

[50]  The church is better off when it has a certain amount of opposition to deal with. It is purified. It recovers the principles of its activity in all their purity. A sleek, fat church, installed in its works, its success, its security, is more likely to become worldly. It may become oblivious of its purpose. It may forget by whom and for whom it exists. . . . The authoritarian regime that has prevailed in the church since the mid-sixteenth century has contributed to the impression that all criticism must auto-

matically proceed from a spirit of hostility, if not indeed from a questionable orthodoxy. A rather limited apologetics, still in use in certain broad Catholic circles, has often thought itself obliged to defend everything *in globo*, applying to the holiness and perfection of the church ideas which are not always exact, and which therefore often cannot be maintained without seeing things differently from the way they really are [Yves M.-J. Congar, *Verdaderas y falsas reformas en la Iglesia* (Madrid, 1953), pp. 122, 24].

> *History's lesson is clear and constant, and St. Columban, whose words were cited at the beginning of Part 2, has given it a gloss. In the church, "the root of all evils is the security of a blind prosperity." ("Omnium malorum causa est caecae prosperitatis securitas.") In light of all that has now been set forth, we surely cannot say that evangelical criticism necessarily impugns the holiness of the church. Sin alone detracts from that holiness. Criticism, provided only it be evangelical, actually edifies, upbuilds, the holiness of the church, by demonstrating that this holiness consists not in an absence of sin in the church, but in the obligation of the church to accept all criticism springing from the gospel. This is how St. Augustine explains the matter in a letter to Jerome, which begins by rejecting the position, held by some, that "it would be better to say that the Gospel is lying than to admit that Peter denied Christ, or to say that the Bible is lying rather than to acknowledge that David committed adultery with Bathsheba." And Augustine cries, "God preserve us!" At the end of his letter he cites the most powerful reason for his position:*

[51]   With all the devotion of a benign humility, Peter accepted the expression of Paul's productive liberty of love. Peter, then, has given an example for all time to come: all ought to allow themselves to be corrected, even by those who are expected to follow them, if perchance the guides should depart from the right path. And this example is even more precious and holy than that of Paul, who invited the small to confront the great courageously, for the defense of the truth of the Gospel, always taking care to safeguard fraternal charity.... For it is more

admirable and praiseworthy to receive correction in good part than peremptorily to correct one who strays [Augustine of Hippo, *Letter 82*, in *Obras* (BAC), 8:508–10].

*In the matter of holiness, then, the official representatives of the church are neither its hierarchs nor its institutions, but only its holy ones. Holiness and ministry, holiness and structure, are not automatically joined together by grace. They are, however, joined together by a greater responsibility and more urgent demand. Accordingly, given the possibility of wicked or anti-evangelical structures, a critical recognition of those structures becomes the path to greater perseverance in unity. After all, at the same time it is very clear in the tradition of the church that the sinfulness of the church never legitimates a "schism" from or breach with that church.*

*Along these same lines we have another testimonial from Augustine's pen:*

[52] I counsel you not to concern yourself unduly about these scandals, which have been foretold precisely in order that, when they come, we may remember that they have been predicted and not be altogether thrown into confusion by them. For the Lord himself said in the Gospel: "Woe to the world from scandals. Scandals must come, yes; but woe to the man by whom a scandal comes" (Matt. 18:7). Whom do you imagine these men to be but the very same as the Apostle describes as "seeking their own interests, not those of Jesus Christ" (Phil. 2:21)? For there are those who occupy pastoral sees for the advantage of Christ's communities, and there are those who occupy them for the sake of their own temporal honor and worldly satisfaction. And these two classes of shepherds will coexist in the church until the end of time. Some will die, but others will be born. . . .

But the Lord has commanded us to continue our journey together, reserving to himself our separation. For only he who cannot err can effect the separation [of what is evil from what is good]. All who have sought, up until now, to separate what the Lord has reserved to himself, have ended by becoming prideful servants, and have only managed to separate themselves from Catholic unity. After all, how can they think to found a pure community if they themselves are stained by schism?

Accordingly—and that we may be able to preserve our unity—the one true Shepherd admonishes us in the Gospel concerning both good shepherds and wicked: concerning the first, that we may strive to imitate their works, but without placing our hope in them—rather glorifying the One who made them such, our Father who is in heaven; and concerning the others, applying to them the name of scribes and Pharisees, who speak well, but whose deeds are wicked [Augustine of Hippo, *Epistolarum Classis III*, Ep. 208 *(PL* 33:950–51)].

> *Criticism, then, when practiced appropriately, asserts the unity of the church. True, it does so in dialectical fashion. It criticizes from within; thus the critic will have to accept the discomfort that comes with being a critic; and thus his or her criticism will be the expression of a concern to avoid a breach. This manner of criticism, as it comes from within, differs radically from criticism made from without. The origin of the latter is typically a wish to destroy, and can readily be transformed into an argument in one's own defense. Criticism from within, far from detracting from the sanctity of the church, actually engages it, sets it in operation—as the following two passages invite us to observe.*

[53]   Our love, our obedience, our silence and our courage, where necessary, profess our belief in the true Church and her spirit of love and freedom to the official representatives of the Church, as did Paul to Peter. And these are much holier and hence always much more powerful realities in the Church than all mediocrity and all the traditionalism which will not believe that our God is the eternal God of all future ages [Karl Rahner, "Thoughts on the Possibility of Belief Today," in *Theological Investigations* (New York: Crossroad, 1982), vol. 5, p. 18].

[54]   The fact that the Christian conscience was scandalized at no longer finding on the chair of Peter the lofty examples it had so frequently admired in the past evinces both a veneration for that see, still intact despite all, and a moral ideal with which compliance was still being demanded [Henri Daniel-Rops, *La*

*Iglesia de los tiempos bárbaros*, p. 577; Eng. trans. of Fr. orig.: *The Church in the Dark Ages* (New York: E. P. Dutton, 1959)].

*In other words, a distinction is made between the church on the one hand, and on the other, such-and-such particular representatives or offices (including the highest) in that church. The critics of earlier days spoke a language which, absurdly, we have lost. The only possible explanation is that our ecclesiology is something less than completely orthodox. And indeed the distinction to which we refer was recommended by St. John Chrysostom long ago, to the tune of some homespun arguments and elementary common sense:*

[55]   Do not blame the priesthood for its unworthy priests. It is not the ministry, but the unworthy minister who is to be blamed. After all, Judas, too, was a traitor. But we do not on that account condemn the whole college of apostles. We simply blame the personal bad conscience of Judas. The evil is not in the priesthood, then, but in the individual conscience [of the priest]. . . . And if someone comes to you and says, "Just look at so-and-so!" you should reply that you prefer to regard not ministers but ministries. After all, think how many physicians have become butchers, administering poisonous drugs rather than healing ones; but we do not on that account attack medicine. We blame the person who abuses medicine. And how many sailors have brought their vessels to shipwreck! But the trouble was in the incompetence of the sailors, not in the fact that they sailed [St. John Chrysostom, *In Illud, Vidi Dominum, Homilia IV* (*PL* 56:126)].

*The distinction is confirmed in the following words of a cardinal of our own day.*

[56]   It is altogether evident from history that there are able shepherds and incompetent ones. For that matter, there are good ones and evil ones. A rabid Catholic, whether or not a member of the hierarchy, can be a mediocre Christian. And while the terminology may be open to discussion, the fact is only too clear from experience: the very thing that paves the way to

holiness also opens the door to the most frightful imposture. . . . All the forms of human wickedness, known and unknown, assume in this case a far more repulsive aspect [Henri de Lubac, *Meditación sobre la Iglesia*, p. 86].

## PERSONAL ASPECTS

A SOCIETY THAT HAS SUBDUED ITS REBELS HAS GAINED ITS PEACE, YES. BUT IT HAS LOST ITS FUTURE [A. de Mello, *El Canto del Pájaro*, p. 197].

*In Part 1, I appealed primarily to the behavior—or critical testimony—of saints or other individuals of irreproachable Christian and ecclesial life. I ignored all criticism directed at the church from without. It is not that I entertain any a priori disregard for such criticism. It is only that I am more interested in the fact of criticism of the church precisely as a Christian phenomenon. Entirely apart from the justice or injustice of their concrete criticisms, the authors of the criticism I have presented were hardly flaming liberals or loveless enemies of the church. On the contrary, many were celebrated precisely for their great love for that church.*

*The first section of the present Part 2 broadened the scope of our reflection. It included a variety of theological elements, not only in the area of ecclesiology (the holiness of the church, its greater responsibility, its need of edification or upbuilding, and its social and human conditions as a great community, where what is whispered is often better shouted from the housetops), but in the matter of that quality of evangelical truth which prohibits it from being hushed up for good (although it may have its opportune and inopportune moments).*

*But these problems are impacted today by yet another factor, and one which sharpens their interest considerably: the rise of modernity, of critical reason, and of human rights. One of the greatest theologians of our times, Karl Rahner, sought to give theology a new foundation in this new context; one place he attempted to do that was in a reflection on the individual (including, where appropriate, the charism of that individual) in the church:*

[57] The freedom of the individual must by no means be regarded as being restricted to a merely private sphere, with no bearing on the community life of the Church: on the contrary, it has a real place in her public life. . . . The fact is that reforms . . . often need the pressure of public opinion if they are not to be stifled by tradition. Even in the higher reaches of the Church, people can believe that all is well because no complaints and no wishes for any sort of change have been heard, or because if they have they seem to be simply isolated views with no weight of public opinion behind them. . . .

Views about the limits to be set to the expressions of this public opinion and the forms it should take will naturally vary considerably when it comes to actual practice. This is bound to happen, because the actual feelings of the various peoples and groups within the Church differ enormously. Some will take some particular expression of opinion as a matter of course, while others will regard it as a tactless criticism, utterly lacking in respect, of Church ordinances and customs. Some will feel frustrated, fearing that pronouncements and explanations always get put off until it is almost too late for them to be of any use. They will feel that a thing is only allowed when in fact it can no longer be stopped, when even the official representatives of the Church have become such children of their own age (but already almost out of date) that the thing they finally sanction and approve is a *fait accompli*, whereas if it had been allowed earlier it would have been the sign of a really liberating and redeeming attitude. Others will regard exactly the same thing as a destructive attack upon sanctified traditions which have established themselves through the wisdom of centuries and proved themselves by long practice to be sound and rich blessings. Exactly the same sort of criticism may be in one case beneficial, or at least harmless, and in another have all the unfortunate consequences expected of it, encouraging an attitude of blasphemy and private rebellion. . . .

The people in the Church (young men in Holy Orders, the laity and so on) must be brought up in a responsible spirit of obedience and be able to make proper use of their right to express their opinions. They must learn that this right to express their own views and to criticize others does not mean licence to

indulge in savage attacks and arrogant presumption. They must
be brought up in a proper critical spirit towards Church matters,
not finding it necessary to rave about anything that happens to
be in favour in the Church at the moment as though it were the
ultimate end of wisdom, and yet able to unite this frame of mind
with a humble and at the same time dignified habit of obedience.
They must learn to unite the inevitable detachment of a critical
public attitude with a genuine and inspired love of the Church
and a genuine subordination and submission to the actual official representatives of the Church. They must learn that even
in the Church there can be a body something like Her Majesty's
Opposition, which in the course of Church history has always
had its own kind of saints in its ranks—the ranks of a genuine,
divinely willed opposition to all that is merely human in the
Church and her official representatives. They must learn—and
this is not just a matter of course, but means a serious effort of
education—that there are circumstances in which people can
have a real duty to speak their minds within the permitted limits
and in a proper spirit of respect, even though this will not bring
them praise and gratitude "from above" (how many examples
there are of this in the history of the saints!). They must also
learn that it can be God's will for them to live for a time, as
Newman said, "under a cloud," because they represent a spirit
out of the ordinary which comes from the Holy Spirit. . . .

Apart from anything else, the Church today should be more
careful than ever before not to give even the slightest impression
that she is of the same order as those totalitarian states for
whom outward power and sterile, silent obedience are everything and love and freedom nothing, and that her methods of
government are those of the totalitarian systems in which public
opinion has become a Ministry of Propaganda. But we—both
those of us who are in authority and those who are under authority—are perhaps still accustomed here and there to certain
patriarchal forms of leadership and obedience which have no
essential or lasting connection with the real stuff of Church
authority and obedience. When this is so, Church authorities
may see even a justifiable expression of frank opinion about
Church matters as camouflaged rebellion, or resentment against
Church Hierarchy. Even those not in authority may dislike such

free expression, because they are accustomed to the old traditional ways. . . .

But compared with the present-day expressions of public
opinion [the] old forms had one outstanding feature: they were
properly drawn up from the legal point of view and formed part
of the layman's rights within the Church. . . . No one would wish
them back again exactly as they were; nevertheless, it is true to
say that there is by comparison very little, if any, recognized way
in which public opinion can make itself felt within the Church
today, according to modern canon law [Karl Rahner, *Free Speech
in the Church* (New York: Sheed and Ward, 1959), pp., 38–39,
48].

*As I have suggested, this passage with its prophetic tones has
its theological foundation in a reflection on the mission of the
individual (indeed, the charism of the individual) in the
church. Elsewhere Rahner takes up these same themes and
emphases:*

[58]   God doesn't abdicate in favour of the Church and leave
her to rule for him undisturbed. . . . When at some future time
it is asked whether we Christians and the Church as she is on
earth today have done the right thing, they will not be able to
say of us that for the most part we have acted theologically
immorally, but perhaps they may not be able to say so easily
that we have done the *will of God*. . . . The chief difficulty when
[Joan of Arc's] cause was brought forward for canonization was
not whether in practice and in theory she was always obedient
to the commands of the Church, but whether, even during her
trial, she ever fell short of this individual duty. . . .

We must distinguish between two functions of conscience:
the one which tells a man's subjective self the *universal* norms
of ethics and moral theology and applies them to his "case,"
and the one by which the individual hears God's call to him
*alone*, which can never be fully deduced from universal
norms. . . . This spiritual and personal uniqueness [of the indi-
vidual] is not subject to universal norms, laws and rules, but
nevertheless . . . is still under the binding will of God, which in
this case is not for the individual as one of a common kind, but

[is] from person to person, from God to each single man. Thus there is a sphere of individual morality and religion, a sphere of moral duties and religious objectives which, while it never conflicts with the universal moral law, nevertheless has the decisive word over and above it and can no longer be contained within it. Of course there is not, and must not be, an individual morality which sets itself up against the universal moral law; but there is an individual morality which is binding on the individual as uniquely for him, and this cannot be called a mere application of a universal principle to one case. ... In every man there is a sphere of personal individuality elevated by grace which we may call *private* and which cannot and may not be touched by the Church. ...

When we are sometimes surprised at people's good will towards the Church and her directives, the leadership of her priests and youth organizers — at least, peoples who are still in regions sociologically Catholic — we should not always be entirely pleased about it; it can also mean an attitude of collectivism, a good will which is not through the power of faith and a vital, carefully considered personal conviction, but a weakness of will which has so little courage and belief in itself that it is ready to follow anyone who is prepared to lead, and in this case it may be the priest because for purely sociological reasons (family tradition, political loyalty etc.), he may be the most immediately obvious leader. But only brave hearts can really be won for God [Karl Rahner, *Nature and Grace: Dilemmas in the Modern Church* (New York: Sheed and Ward, 1964), pp. 34, 31–32, 30, 20, 19, 23, 29].

[59]   There are, in fact, earnest Catholics who are anxious to have a right mind about the Church and who hold the view, tacitly and in the background, but all the more operative and dangerous on that account, that the hierarchy is the only vehicle of the Spirit or the only portal through which the Spirit enters the Church. They imagine the Church as a sort of centralized state, and a totalitarian one at that. We must distinguish between what we may perhaps for our present purpose call an absolute claim made by the Church, valid within certain limits and strictly circumscribed, and a totalitarian conception of the Church.

For the Catholic the Church is absolute in the sense that he knows that the Church is the enduring and imperishable home of his salvation. . . . But this attribution of an absolute character does not involve a totalitarian view of the Church. Such a conception would be totalitarian if anyone were to think, explicitly or tacitly, that the Church is not liable to err in any of her actions, if it were supposed that all living impulses of the Church can and may only originate from her official ministers, that any initiative in the Church is only legitimate if it springs expressly or at least equivalently from above and only after it has been authorized, that all guidance of the Holy Spirit always and in every case affects ecclesiastical office, God directing his Church only through her hierarchy and that every stirring of life in the Church is the mere carrying out of an order or a wish "from above." Such a false totalitarian view inevitably equates office and charisma, if any importance is left to this latter. But this is just what is not the case. For there are charismata, that is, the impulsion and guidance of God's Spirit for the Church, in addition to and outside her official ministry. . . .

If the structure of the Church is of this double kind and if her harmonious unity is ultimately guaranteed only by the one Lord, then office-holders and institutional bodies must constantly remind themselves that it is not they alone who rule in the Church. We have already sufficiently emphasized that God's Spirit will ensure that they do not rule in that way and in decisive matters will not wish to do so. But this fact in no way means that temptations to the contrary never arise or that such a maxim is superfluous because its final accomplishment is guaranteed. Neither the efficacious grace given in God's salvific acts nor the indefectible promise to the Church of the assistance of the Holy Spirit renders such a maxim superfluous. It is important for office-holders and their subjects, too, to keep it clearly before their minds. Both must realize that in the Church which has this charismatic element, subordinates are quite definitely not simply people who have to carry out orders from above. They have other commands as well to carry out, those of the Lord himself who also guides his Church directly and does not always in the first place convey his commands and promptings to ordinary Christians through the ecclesiastical authorities, but has entirely reserved for himself the right to do this directly in a great variety of ways that have little to do with keeping to the standard procedure and the "usual channels." . . . There are actions that God wills even before the starting signal has been given by the hierarchy, and in directions that have not yet been positively approved and laid down officially. Canon law concerning equity and the force of custom *contra* or *praeter legem* might be thought out from the point of view of this charismatic element in the Church. By such concepts canonists not only leave legitimate room for humanly significant development in the law, but also for the impulse of the Spirit, even if and in spite of the fact that these points in the Church's body can also, of course, become the focus of infection by the all-too-human element. . . . [Executive authority] must keep alive the consciousness that it is a duty and not a gracious condescension when it accepts suggestions from "below"; that it must not from the start pull all the strings; and that the higher and, in fact, charismatic wisdom can sometimes be with the subordinate, and that the charismatic wisdom of office may consist in not shutting itself off from such higher wisdom. . . .

If by her very nature there is necessarily a multiplicity of impulsions in the Church, then a legitimate opposition of forces is not only, in fact, unavoidable, but is to be expected and must be accepted by all as something that should exist. It is not just to be regarded as a necessary evil. . . . Ultimately only one thing can give unity in the Church on the human level: the love which allows another to be different, even when it does not understand him. . . . The principle that charity brings with it implies that each in the Church may follow his spirit as long as it is not established that he is yielding to what is contrary to the Spirit; that, therefore, orthodoxy, freedom and goodwill are to be taken for granted and not the opposite. Those are not only self-evident human maxims of a sensible common life built on respect and tolerance for others, but also principles which are very deeply rooted in the very nature of the Church and must be so. For they follow from the fact that the Church is not a totalitarian system. Patience, tolerance, leaving another to do as he pleases as long as the error of his action is not established — and not the other way round, prohibition of all individual initiative until its legitimacy has been formally proved, with the onus of proof laid on the subordinate — are, therefore, specifically ecclesiastical virtues springing from the very nature of the Church [Karl Rahner, *The Dynamic Element in the Church* (New York: Herder and Herder, 1964), pp. 48, 49, 69–71, 73, 74, 75, 76, 77, 78, 79–81].

# PART III

# THE NORMS

Ever seeking not one's own interests, but those of Christ
(Phil. 2:21)

# TEXTS WITH COMMENTARY

*Having established the fact of criticism in the church, then its justification, we are now confronted with a third task. Notwithstanding all that has been said, not all criticism of the church is legitimate or valid. In order to be such, it must fulfill certain conditions. It will be highly useful to examine these conditions if we hope to deal with the fact of criticism in the church. We must not reject that criticism in principle. But we must appraise it for its compliance or noncompliance with these conditions. The requisites in question cannot be enunciated with mathematical precision. After all, they are principles for the solution of a human question. Nevertheless, they are absolutely necessary. The mere fact that criticism may be illegitimate or invalid does not render it harmless. And the mortal danger of illegitimate criticism does not lie in its intent to manipulate the church according to a critic's whim. It lies in the risk of falling victim to an attitude of irreverent superiority. St. Cyran, the father of Jansenism, a person haunted by a deep religious obsession, betrayed this irreverent superiority when he declared: "God has given me to know that, for five or six hundred years now, there has been no Church."*

*We shall launch our search for the criteria of legitimate criticism in the church by presenting a digest of an article written forty years ago by a German Jesuit. It constitutes a veritable mini-treatise on the conditions for legitimate criticism of the church.*

## [60] I. REQUISITES FOR A LEGITIMATE CRITICISM

The justification for a criticism of the human element in the church, in its representatives and institutions, resides in the very essence of that church. Here, in most intimate fashion, the divine and the human cross paths. And so only one question remains. What characteristics must criticism have in order to be genuinely constructive—truly "edifying," upbuilding, with respect to the church? . . . What conditions are necessary in order for a criticism of the church to be genuinely fruitful and enhancing for its life? This article will be concerned with a response to these questions.

1. The first and indispensable condition for the legitimacy of criticism in the church is an *authentic love of the church*. . . . Are not love and criticism incompatible? How can we love something, and then attack and fight it? The answer is very simple. A mother correcting her child knows very well that love and reprimand go hand in hand. The one springs precisely from the other. A zealous love can be manifested in reprimand. The picture of her child that the mother bears in her heart— the picture of what the child ought to be— conflicts with the image the child presents in reality. . . . And the mother's perception of the distance between the "ought to be" and the "is" of the child is the occasion of the reprimand, whose only purpose is to bring the "is" up to the "ought to be."

Something similar occurs in the case of the believer and the church. Of course, this time the relationship is reversed. The loving child stands before his mother. His faith tells him "how the church should be" in the intention and will of Christ. At the same time he contemplates the weakness of so many of its members, so many dried-up wellsprings of life, the devastation of so many "holy places"— all the things that have filled the history of the church for two thousand years. Then love lifts its voice, in behalf of the divine element in the church and against what is "too human" in the same, and seeks to heal its ailing members, rescue the wellsprings, and halt the corruption. Such a love may permit itself all the accents of zeal: anger, accusation, cry and castigation, storming and imprecation. One thing alone is forbidden. It may not reject the church. It may not forget the divine element in the church, transcending the human aspect. It may not withdraw from the church in a spirit of self-justification and scandal-taking. In the midst of all their criticism of the church, the Catholic faithful hold *mordicus* to their posture as its children: a posture of respect and gratitude, devotion and obedience, unquestioned loyalty come what may. This was the attitude of the saints and the true reformers. This is the attitude of those who take their profession of Catholic faith seriously. . . .

2. The second requisite for the legitimacy of a criticism of the church is a courageous, authentic *liberty*. It is not only the church hierarchy who must demonstrate this liberty, this freedom. Anyone may voice his or her criticism in the church of God, provided the difficult, but indispensable conditions we are listing be observed. If the hierarchy is in some manner central to the church, the majority of the great reformers were truly "marginal" elements, whose activity flowed not from the charge of their ministry, but from the force of their personality. . . .

But all of this is in precious little evidence today. So much criticism of the church has little or nothing of the liberty, the freedom of which we are speaking. First there is anonymous criticism, which lacks the courage of a personal commitment— a commitment of one's own person—in behalf of its claims. Obviously such a procedure is condemned to failure. And yet experience teaches us that anonymous criticism is as deathless in the church as the spiritual attitude from which it springs. Second, and along with the first, comes another sort of criticism that can scarcely pride itself on its daring of spirit: rumor and whispering—criticism mumbled from ear to ear, and to every ear but that of its object. . . . It was a consummation devoutly to be wished that all critics would swear never to say behind the back of others what they would not dare say to their face. At least this would eliminate that revolting brand of criticism that consists in censuring in victims' absence what one praises in their presence! . . .

3. Even more important is a third requirement: *justice.* . . . Criticism can easily fall prey to the temptation to exempt itself from the demands of justice. After all, it springs from a zeal for good, and the critic can unconsciously feel that the end justifies the means. Rarely will a mighty zeal for good be sufficiently even-tempered and lucid not to fire at least somewhat sporadically, despite all good intentions. What is desired, then, is a healthy dose of self-control and sense of responsibility. This would avoid the harm that can befall when would-be constructive criticism offends against justice. . . . The most typical failing in this area consists in an invalid generalization from a particular set of observations and facts . . . or hasty conclusions concerning

a given state of affairs without the benefit of familiarity with the overall context and background.

4. But in addition to justice, criticism must have another quality if it is to have the best chance of reaching its objective: *good sense....* [This is a matter of talent.] What we mean when we say that a person has a talent for doing something is that he or she has the ability, taking all circumstances into account, to find the means most readily conducive to the desired end. In the case before us, the desired end is the elimination of defects and failings. If our sole concern is the manifestation of our annoyance or disenchantment in some particular matter, then, of course, we need have no talent. But anyone who takes the holiness of the church very seriously will have many questions that only an authentically Christian sagacity will be able to answer.

Far from having no bearing on the practical outcome, the moment chosen for the criticism, the person who is to voice it, its audience, its object, the manner in which it is expressed, and its degree or intensity, may actually be decisive for that outcome. In a matter of such delicacy, one small detail neglected, one piece of carelessness and unconcern, may spoil a great undertaking. The same detail, well managed, can work miracles. Care and tact never harmed anyone. Neither have they ever worked to the detriment of justifiable criticism. But the absence of tact, the neglect of politeness and amenity, just as other failings of respect and sensitivity, are pernicious in the extreme....

Does this mean that criticism must be smothered in an overdose of prudence and precaution? Not at all. It merely means that our criticism must conform to the advice given us by St. Ambrose—that we "seek not to be a victor, but a physician." A good physician will consider very carefully whether, and where, the scalpel should be applied, or whether, instead, some other therapy is indicated.

5. Accordingly, any authentically Catholic criticism of the church must meet a final, absolutely indispensable requirement: that of *humility*.

Wherever criticism is expressed, the opportunity for a practice of humility will be abundant. The very resistance almost surely to be offered, rightly or wrongly—more likely, both rightly and wrongly—to any effort of reform or renewal will be a call to humility. We need only recall the celebrated struggles waged by the reformers of religious orders throughout history. How protracted these struggles, and how uncertain their outcome! Add to this the fact that criticism will have its own shortcomings, as it will rarely meet all the requirements of our ideal picture, and we can scarcely doubt that criticism will stir up storms of internal oppression such as only a sincere humility will be able to weather. But the sacrifices that the critic will have to make may be as useful for the end in view as the criticism itself. . . .

## [61]  II. CONDITIONS FOR RECEIVING CRITICISM

In the second place, we must now ask: what is required of the addressee of criticism? What precautions must be taken lest the critical utterance fall by the wayside, and lie stifled and fruitless?

1. The first requirement will be that of *openness to criticism*. The object or addressee of the criticism must be possessed of a receptivity proper to that same Christian humility that we demand as the last condition of criticism itself. . . . The more lively that spirit of humility in the church—the humility of its Founder—the better off the church will be. And a great deal more humility is needed for an honest acknowledgment of public faults, or faults that become common knowledge by way of criticism, than is needed to admit them to oneself privately. By way of compensation, however, an acknowledgment of the truth is the most powerful response to exaggerated accusations.

2. In the second place, especially in the Catholic case, a certain *security and tranquility* is required in the face of criticism, both general criticism of the church and criticism of particular aspects. Not a few Catholics—often enough the best of them—regard all criticism, especially public criticism, with insecurity and anxiety. They reject it out of hand. They close their minds to it, as if all criticism were necessarily an attack on the very holiness of the church. Surely there are instances of vitriolic, totally baseless criticism that calls for outright rejection by Catholics—criticism that does indeed impugn the very essence and sanctity of the church. But not even in these cases need a Catholic tremble for that church. We ought to know that the church

is indestructible by the will of Christ, and we have abundant evidence of this down through all the two thousand years of its history, a history that continues today. . . . Castles in the air are of cloud, and will pass with the clouds. And no cloud lasts two thousand years. . . . For four centuries now, the demise of the church has been reported by serious observers at least once each century. And yet the church lives. . . .

Accordingly, we need not regard criticism as automatically unthinkable in the church of God, or that criticism is necessarily harmful to the healthy development of that church. The worst times for the church were not those of a lively activity of minds anxious for its reform, bitter though the struggle might be. The worst times for the church were those in which — as at the waning of the Middle Ages — none any longer dared mount an effective criticism of unbridled corruption. Potential critics had all succumbed to a sense of helplessness in the face of a seemingly overwhelming reality. Criticism made in all seriousness was received in a cavalier or mocking way, so that long-repressed dissatisfaction was bottled up, to explode all at once in the Reformation, in the form of criticism that had gone beyond all bounds.

The Third Reich has given us a flagrant example of how destructive the absence of criticism — and concretely, of public criticism — can be for any community entity. And may this example suffice for a long time to come. . . . May the day never dawn for the Catholic Church when persons filled with an authentic desire for reform will find even the slightest pretext for having recourse to anonymous criticism on the grounds that there was simply no other way to voice their anxiety. . . .

But is not all of this a dangerous game? Can criticism not injure the image of the church in the eyes of "outsiders"? The question is an honest one. But we do not think it has a great deal of importance. The time is past when real shortcomings might possibly be concealed by way of a system of deceit and fraud (as, once more, in the classic instance of the events and conditions during the time of the Third Reich). The case is just the other way about. Where there are believers who make a serious, responsible effort in behalf of the purity of their church and its assimilation to Christ, such behavior will always be taken seriously by serious persons, as experience attests. As for the voices of those whose intent is scandal at any cost, the church need pay them no heed in any case.

3. Last, we must maintain the greatest possible *objectivity*, and *justice*, cost what it may, vis-à-vis all criticism. The greater our willingness to leave personal considerations out of account and attend solely to the question at hand, the more the tone of our response will be one of self-control and justice, instead of agitation and lust for victory. And there will be far more hope of actually settling the matters under dispute, of actually correcting any defects that may be present, without injuring the image of the church either in the eyes of its members or in those of "outsiders."

We sincerely believe that if discussions on the life of the church were pursued on the terrain we have outlined, the church could only emerge from them enriched and blessed [A. Koch, "Kritik an der Kirche," *Stimmen der Zeit* 141 (1947–48):169–84].

•

*Although the article condensed above is an adequate and complete presentation in itself, it will be worthwhile to observe that one of the requisites it lists for a valid criticism of the church has often been discussed — and experienced — by other persons of the church. What Koch has called humility is something that can be practiced only if we set no limits on it — only if we practice it in the acceptance of a radical aloneness and an at least initial rejection. This is prophets' fate, this is the crucible where love for the church is purified and tried by fire. Legitimate criticism is more painful for the critic than for anyone else, not only because the critic is included in its object, but by reason of the number of ultimately unnecessary "complications" it occasions. In one of his homilies on Ezekiel, Origen exclaims in astonishment:*

[62]   What is it then that I admire in Ezekiel? It is that when he was commanded to give witness and to "make known to Jerusalem her abominations" (Ezek. 16:2), he did not put before his eyes the danger that could come from this preaching but,

mindful only of fulfilling God's command, he spoke all that he
was told to speak. Certainly it is a mystery, it is the revelation
of a sanctified understanding about Jerusalem and about all the
things said of her. And yet he prophetically accuses her of "fornication" because "she spread her legs to everyone who passed
by" (Ezek. 16:15, 25). He attests this with condemnatory voice,
he excoriates the city for its wickedness [in Hans Urs von Balthasar, ed., *Origen: Spirit and Fire* (Washington, D.C.: Catholic
University of America Press, 1984), p. 160].

*The words Ezekiel speaks to Jerusalem are applied by Origen
to the church. Jerusalem's salvation comes last, after that of
Sodom and Samaria ("the pagans and heterodox") — because
"the closer we are to God, the further we remove ourselves
from him when we sin." Hans Urs von Balthasar makes the
following commentary on Origen's words:*

[63]    Origen uses a very prudent, moderate language here. He
speaks of the representatives of the church, not of the church
as such. But he speaks of these representatives precisely as representatives of the church, and precisely in proportion as they
are representatives of the church. He nearly always refers to
those who, by reason of their ministry, are representatives and
exhibitors of the church, and does not excuse them, any more
than the prophet excused Jerusalem the prostitute.

But at the same time, Origen speaks in existential fashion.
He must speak of himself in these homilies. For the church
would be more pure if he were not so impure. Here as in other
passages . . . Origen takes the last place, as the most unworthy
of all, accepting the entire blame for the very shortcomings he
criticizes. On the strength of this authentic gesture, he is able
to convince other believers that the greatest sin, the ultimate
sin, is to be found in "Jerusalem": in the representatives of the
church. And the latter are all the more guilty the more they,
like the Pharisees, pride themselves on their ecclesiastical purity
and wisdom [Hans Urs von Balthasar, *Ensayos Teológicos* (Madrid, 1964), 2:315–16].

*Cardinal Ratzinger, in his commentary on a text of Gerhoh
of Reichersberg, whom I have cited in Part 1, regards the*

*dilemma of criticism in the church as an opportunity to express
one's true love for that church.*

[64]   Is it an unqualified sign of better times that theologians
today no longer dare to speak in this tone? Is it not rather a
sign of diminished love, and of a heart no longer on fire with
holy zeal for the cause of God in this world (2 Cor. 11:2), a love
that has become dull, and that no longer dares embrace suffering for the beloved and for the sake of the beloved? The one
who no longer feels the defection of a friend, who no longer
suffers for that friend, and who no longer struggles for that
friend's return—such a one no longer loves. Is this not applicable to our relationship with the church? [Josef Ratzinger, *El
nuevo pueblo de Dios* (Barcelona, 1972), p. 290].

*This may well be the key to our paradox. There is such a thing
as a love whose object is dearer to the lover than peace and
tranquility. A love like that will actually be willing to embrace
suffering for the sake of the beloved. This is the love that ought
to, and could, characterize criticism in the church. I believe I
have seen such love. It is not a matter of pure theory, then. I
think I have seen it in Karl Rahner, whose words have appeared so often in this book. On this account, and in homage
to the great teacher who has recently left us, I should like to
close the present inquiry with a few paragraphs from the eulogy
pronounced at Father Rahner's funeral by Alfons Klein, Provincial of the Jesuits of southern Germany. Part of that eulogy
was a lengthy passage on Rahner as a person of the church.*

[65]   The point of departure of Father Rahner's theology was
the core and center of the human being. This is what lent such
credibility to his discourse. But on not a few occasions it also
rendered that discourse a critical, admonishing, and angry one,
especially when he had the impression that certain procedures
in the church, instead of permitting the uninhibited contemplation of God, God's love for us, and God's mercy, interfered with
that contemplation. For Father Rahner, as for St. Ignatius, the
motto *sentire cum ecclesia* did not denote an uncritical acceptance of what was handed down from above, so that any respon-

sibility would be shifted upwards, and the responsibility of the subject would be merely to hear and to comply. No, it meant *sentire* — that is, thinking, feeling with the church. But the church exists for human beings, not the other way around. Therefore *sentire cum ecclesia* will mean thinking and feeling with human beings, as well. Human beings' problems touched his heart, and he expressed the needs of persons as a person of frank word and deep sensitivity, in the name of the suffering, the questioning, and the desperate.

Again like Ignatius, Karl Rahner lived a basic dynamic tension. On the one side, he fully acknowledged the unbounded aspect of the church, even in its human form and with all its limitations. He accepted the church as God has accepted us in the incarnation of Jesus — whole and entire, with all our sins and weaknesses.

On the other side, the church for him was not God. It was a pathway to God. It was a means, a provisional, transitory instance, whose task and justification consisted in the finality that Jesus had established for it: to make room for God, and to actualize for human beings God's love and mercy — to serve men and women along their journey through this life to God.

And so when he saw the church in danger of swerving from its mission, he spoke out, and he did so frankly and courageously. He could show the anger of the prophet, the anger of one wounded in his great love for the church and humanity. And so he was a thorn in the churchly flesh. And this explains his suffering for the cause of the church.

Yet he never revoked his "yes" to the concrete church. He remained faithful to that church, somewhat as a good spouse may remain faithful to a marriage even at the most difficult, tension-charged times. And whatever he did, he did for love of the church and for human beings. He did everything out of a sense of responsibility for the church and for the human beings toward whom he felt the obligations of a servant of the good news of Jesus.

He could be critical, then. But his interest was always in the church in its overall dimension. His words never echoed with the vanity of a know-it-all. They were fueled by the exclusive desire that the greatest possible number of men and women should understand the good news of the redemption of Jesus Christ and experience it as salvation.

When he was the object of a criticism that issued from the church itself, he was pained. Especially in his last years, as it gradually came to be "open season on Rahner" in certain circles in the church, he was frequently attacked by persons who either had not read him at all, or, if they had, had not grasped his intent, ranging from the highly placed to the simple. He was criticized and vilified. He received insulting letters. He read them. He kept them. They affected and pained him.

He could bear criticism as far as his person, or some particular tenet of his, was concerned. He was humble enough to accept justified criticism, and devout enough to accept unjustified criticism, like Jesus, or like his Father Ignatius. What pained him was the thought of having somehow failed in Jesus' service. He had a very delicate conscience in this respect. He sought to serve men and women, not to inflict harm on them. Consequently criticism affected him deeply. He had the impression that he was being reproached with a lack of love for the church. After all, here he was being told that he was destroying the church, that he was a heretic, that he was confusing and disorienting the faithful. Of course he had sought to do nothing of the kind. His only intent had been to serve the church and human beings. But, however absurd the criticism might seem— and on more than one occasion it was completely absurd— Father Rahner was never so sure of himself, or so possessed of a sense of superiority, as to exclude the possibility that, despite his best intentions, he had indeed fallen into certain errors or made certain mistakes.

Toward the end of his life, however, as he looked back over the years, he managed to relativize this painful experience. And he could be heard to say to younger colleagues who were deeply disturbed at being attacked and criticized, "Oh, it's not that serious."

Another of Father Rahner's Ignatian traits was his faculty for the discernment of spirits. Totally orientated toward God, he possessed a fine sense—a "nose," as his brother Hugo called it—for judging all else beside. From the distance of the transcendent, on the basis of the interior liberty that arises when one refuses to confound God with anything finite, and takes God alone as one's foundation, he found that he could be open to everything. He could listen, he could learn, he could avoid hasty judgments. And so he had tolerance and serenity. He was able to recognize good; and like his Father Ignatius, he presupposed good in every individual, even when he had to begin to bring that individual to the light by way of a patient hearing (*Spiritual Exercises*, no. 22). Simultaneously, this same exclusive orientation toward God endowed him with the capacity to discern obstacles along the path to God and human beings—even when a given obstacle was couched in religious terminology and thereby represented all the greater danger to human beings. Then Karl Rahner would speak out!

# PART IV

# HERE AND NOW

## Wrinkle of Authoritarianism, Blemish of Wealth (cf. Eph. 5:25–27)

> *You must bear in mind that, if I speak strongly in various places ... against the existing state of things [in the church], it is not wantonly, but to show I feel the difficulties which certain minds are distressed with [John Henry Cardinal Newman, letter to J. Keble, September 6, 1843].*

# DISSENT PAST AND PRESENT

*Before presenting some brief reflections on this compilation of texts from so many authors, it may be useful to draw up a kind of synthesis or balance sheet of the content of those texts. (Throughout, I shall refer to the texts by the numeral that appears at the beginning of each.)*

## 1. BALANCE SHEET: SYNTHESIS OF THE TEXTS

We see that our texts fall naturally into two very different moments in the history of the church. Some were written before, and others after, the Council of Trent and the inception of the Tridentine reform. Thus our balance sheet will be drawn up roughly in terms of each half, respectively, of this second millennium of Christian history.

### 1.1. Pre-Tridentine Texts

#### A. Point of Departure for the Criticism

A first characteristic of the older, pre-Tridentine, texts is the point of reference from which the criticism is made. We can formulate this point of departure in a manner that will surely be most meaningful and useful to us today. *The church is criticized from the standpoint of the gospel, and not merely from that of the prevailing cultural ambiance.* (Note the abundance of scriptural references in these earlier texts.) Doubtless this is owing at least in part to the phenomenon of Christendom. But this explanation seems inadequate. After all, Christendom, too, knew established, non-evangelical attitudes and behaviors. The church was all but forced to assimilate these, along with the gospel, and this is precisely what its prophets criticize. Let us consider a single example of the theology of church ministry in our texts. As implied in the first of our texts, by St. Bernard, that theology might be summarized as follows: the *raison d'être* of the ecclesial ministry is the flock, not the ministry itself. Still less are the sheep for the sake of the shepherd, although they were being treated as if they were. Granted, *evangelical* criticism will frequently be "utopian." But precisely on that account the response, "Things have never been that way," is automatically invalidated (see text 2).

The evangelical character of criticism in the church entails a number of important consequences.

1. First, criticism from the standpoint of the gospel will be *permanent and ongoing*. It will be obsessed with a purity that is eschatological, and, therefore, impossible to satisfy. It is a heart-rending obsession. And yet this discourse does not for all that leave off, or lapse into resignation. As we have so often had the occasion to observe, the gospel refuses to leave the church in peace.

2. In the second place, the evangelical point of reference also *justifies* criticism. The gospel belongs to all of the faithful, and not just to the hierarchy. If St. Catherine is bold enough to address the "sweet Christ of the earth," it is because she speaks "on behalf of the Christ of heaven" (see text 7 and the commentary that follows 7). In other words, Catherine recognizes that each and every member of the faithful, even a lowly nun in her twenties, possesses something of the Spirit—something of the "Christ of heaven." Not even the pope can change that. Therefore, she knows, her personal freedom on the one side and her love for the community of the church on the other can coincide in critical discourse, instead of being mutually opposed there.

3. Again in virtue of the gospel reference point, criticism, even in its quality as discourse upon responsibility, *is not directed toward hierarchs alone*, as if it sprang from some sort of Freudian anti-authoritarianism. No, the faithful, too, the "doctor" caste (theologians!), and the very critic, become the object of the criticism (see text 10). And as it springs from a concern for responsibility, criticism in the church becomes a perennial demand that the responsibility in question never be discharged to the advantage of the person responsible (or even to the advantage of that one's position or function). That responsibility may be

discharged only as a modality of "proexistence" — only as service to the community and the gospel.

4. Finally, it is again in virtue of the evangelical point of reference that criticism possesses its *redemptive potential*. A criticism made from a point of departure in the gospel assumes and presupposes that, despite the sorry state of reality, (1) the pope is still our father, and may not allow himself to reject our criticism out of pridefulness (text 25); and that (2) the faithful are still church — that is, actually responsible for the church, and not disinterested observers or outside agitators, let alone seekers after grandeur at the church's expense. It likewise assumes that the pope and faithful are always more closely united by the exigencies of the gospel than they are divided by their hypothetical confrontation (see text 25).

Together with this reference to the gospel (or rather by way of concretizing this reference), several of our texts have cited the practice of the primitive church (see texts 2, 18, 19, 20, 31, and passim). The primitive church corresponds to a privileged moment in theological tradition. Here we must be careful to make the crucial distinction between authentic tradition, which is theological, and traditionalism, which is sociological. Traditionalism, while it formally appeals to "tradition," almost never refers materially to the primitive church. Its reference is nearly always to a time immediately preceding some great historical change. It is a datum abundantly confirmed by the experience of our own day that the people who most appeal to "tradition" actually have in mind only the last century, or, at the earliest, the range of centuries between the Councils of Trent and Vatican II.

The evangelical reference constitutes an important lesson for modern critics of the church. Not surprisingly, much of the criticism directed against the church today — even by Christians — emerges from the cultural demands of modernity. This circumstance is scarcely censurable in itself. The gospel is *always* read from a point of departure in a culture; and the Spirit of Jesus *also* (along with human sinfulness) affects the march of cultures in history, often succeeding in transforming them into the locus of the divine generation of an evangelical truth that God's people have sinfully forgotten. (And this may explain why, with the coming of the modern age and the collapse of Christendom, the evangelical reference is less explicitly invoked in our post-Tridentine texts.)

But none of this militates against the urgency of the cultural values of any given history themselves being subjected to criticism from the standpoint of the gospel before a Christian may present them to the church in the form of a critical demand. Once more we find ourselves dealing with what is called the hermeneutic circle. It is dangerous in the extreme to attempt to break out of this circle in favor of a one-way street. Just because the gospel is the wisdom of God for us, it does not therefore cease to be insanity and scandal for anything "Greek" or "Jewish" any of us may still be clinging to (see 1 Cor. 1:22–23). That is, the gospel persists in being critical of those historically and culturally rooted values that are frequently employed in criticism of the church. Thus for example it will be legitimate to ask whether some of the demands thrown at the church today in the area of sexual morality spring from the liberty of the gospel or from the libertinage of a pagan milieu that is unconscious (as in Rom. 1:18ff.) of its own sin and that is contaminating Christian criticism as well. Likewise it will be legitimate to ask whether criticism of the exercise of authority in the church may perhaps arise simply out of the modern notion of democracy, rather than out of the New Testament concept of "communion" or *koinonia*. To be sure, today we must add that the historical notion of democracy offers an incomparably superior incarnation of evangelical *koinonia* than do the historical notions of absolute monarchy or aristocracy. But aristocracy is no obstacle to the *concrete reality* of what we call democracy, and the mentalities generated by democracy must be criticized from the standpoint of the gospel (as also simply from that of the human being).

### B. Themes of Criticism

The second trait that I wish to single out is thematic in nature. We cannot help being struck by the key importance of two themes in nearly all of our texts. First, there is the subject of wealth, which invariably immediately entails a discourse on the poor. Second, there is authority and power. Obviously these are not the only objects of criticism in our texts. But I shall concentrate on these, because they pervade the whole chronology of this survey, as well as because they serve so well as a basis for reflection today.

*B1. Poverty and Wealth.* Criticism in the area of poverty and wealth appears at once in this anthology, in texts 1, 2, 3, and 5 by St. Bernard. Like the dust of the road that clings to the traveler's shoes, the culture of St. Bernard's time had clung to the church, and the wealth that was part and parcel of that culture disfigured the texture of that church, perverting relationships among its members. Its hierarchs were distributors of "favors," rather than brothers. Hence a relationship with them would immediately tend to degenerate into a relationship of self-interest (text 2). Our authors tend to see something more than personal or occasional sin here. While we may not always speak of "structural" sin, we must indeed say that our critics see *structured* sin here. That is, they discern deleterious usages or customs that have congealed and established themselves. It is precisely for this reason, incidentally, that these usages are open to descriptions of such luxuriant detail. More importantly, this is why they can be criticized without impugning the good will of the persons who comprise their collective subject. But finally, this is also why they remain ambiguous—or are even accounted a blessing!—or at least are not always clearly seen and forthrightly condemned (see text 6).

This theme, furthermore, is one of those that provoke the harshest criticism (see texts 1–5, 6, 11, 22). The reason is given repeatedly, and is abundantly clear: *the poor are the sovereigns of the church and the criterion of its identity.* Hence the towering importance of the sensibility *of* the poor, as well as of sensitivity *to* the poor (texts 2, 6, 20). The goods of the church are the property of the poor, our critics constantly repeat (6, 9, 11, 21), and the gospel will not tolerate the church's dissipation of the goods of the poor in behalf of particular interests, or interests alien from those of the poor. Gold may not be preferred to Christ. The accumulation of benefices (20, 21, 23, 26) and the default of a community of goods in the church (20) may not be allowed to leave the poor helpless and exposed (23). Otherwise the simple will look down on the church, despise it (20). Furthermore, such abuses of private ownership degenerate into something like a "class struggle" in the church (23). The other side of the coin is that wealth leads to absolutism, and the latter to a corruption of ministries in the form of "favors," careerism, and the like (2, 12, 23, 26, etc.).

This same state of affairs is presented by Rosmini (31), and not in a purely descriptive or enunciative manner, but together with a disclosure of the process leading to it, after the fashion of a master of spirituality seeking to unmask some temptation of the evil one. The steps in this imperceptible process are more or less as follows. An excess of ambivalent means (money, power, and so on) has led to practices contrary to the gospel; these practices have in turn occasioned a gradual increase in the use of these same means; and so on in a vicious circle.

Finally, in the most recent texts (but still antedating Vatican II), this theme is expressed in formulations very different from those of a St. Bernard. The personal behavior of the addressees of criticism is no longer so reprehensible, then. Now discourse on this theme more closely resembles that destined to prevail especially in the aftermath of Vatican II: allegations of an absence of social commitment or want of justice (33), of an alliance with the mighty against the poor (41), and so on. But the theological interest is the same as in the ancient texts.

*B2. Authority.* In the matter of authority, our texts present a double series of criticisms. The first is directed against an *image* of authority, which, by way of the accumulation of wealth, has been contaminated by the image of worldly authority.[1] The second is directed against an *absolutist manner of exercising* authority. The second series of criticisms seems to derive from the first; in any case we are struck by the parallelism between these two series and the great passage from Luke 22 (25ff.) concerning lords of the earth who are styled benefactors and yet who oppress their subjects. We likewise see that, if we attempted to formulate both series in positive rather than negative terms—in terms of the ideal implied in the criticism—they would yield a veritable spiritual treatise on the practice of authority in the church, which would embrace three points.

a. Authority in the church should have the overtones not of the "dignity" of the world (text 2), but of the genuine dignity revealed by God in the gospel, which consists in "becoming flesh" to dwell among human beings (John 1:14). For St. Bernard, therefore, the papacy, in itself as in its relationship with the other churches, ought to constitute a materialization of this utopian trait proper to the church rather than a polarizing element of ecclesial structure (text 2). Yet a Gerhoh will dare to present, not the papacy, it is true, but the Roman Curia of his time, as a veritable paragon of that "mundanization" of the image of authority (13) which will ultimately occasion the sarcastic observation, "yesterday the church, today the Curia."

This evangelical notion of dignity implies an obligation to avoid all contagion of certain worldly images of dignity, according to which the latter would reside in a wealth of appearances (1, 5, 6, 12, 21). If the authority of the church embraces this falsified image, it will inevitably couple with the powers of this world (13, 15, 19, 23), and even with the least evangelical of these powers, as those hostile to the poor ("the conservatives" [33] and "the mighty" [41]). Confronted with the peril of this self-encumbrance, ecclesiastical authority must endeavor to assume the image of the one who held himself out "as an ordinary human being" (Phil. 2:9). In other words, ecclesial authority must have no fear of manifesting its human condition (text 21). Otherwise it will be "stealing the key of authority," as St. Bernard puts it (4).

b. A like assimilation to the worldly image of authority will necessarily occasion a series of concrete usages which in an evangelical perspective are of course to be avoided. Our texts decry the following (among others):

—An absence of freedom on the part of this authority, which will be commandeered by those with whom it shares its worldly image. This will issue precisely in a deprivation of *real* authority, and the official church will find itself sterile and isolated at the very moment when it is most concerned to assert its power (38).

—Absolutism. The human being cannot be everything (20). Any attempt to ignore this fact will result in an excessive centralization, and thereby prevent the accumulation of sufficient, and sufficiently reliable, information to serve as a basis for action (20).

—Abuses in making appointments to church offices (2, 10,

21). For example, such appointments will often be made in view of a "good social position" in the world (6), or an alliance of church policy with worldly interests (31).

— The abuse of spiritual power (21, 23), which will often be employed to silence the prophetic voices themselves (1, 3, 13). Incidentally, this will redound to the discredit of those practicing the abuse (23).

— A focus on many things that are extraneous to the norm of faith — rules, norms, and ideals springing simply from established usage. These will be stubbornly defended as "of faith," or at least as somehow inviolable (25). The Papal States are not the sole example.

— The utilization of collaborators or subordinates to assume responsibility for decisions not their own — decisions actually emanating from a higher authority — for the purpose of safeguarding the anonymity, and thereby the image, of that higher authority (39).

c. Finally, some of our texts call attention to the taproot of all the dangers that lurk in what Dante called "confounding two modes of rule" (15) — a confusion sometimes personified in allusions to Constantine or Charlemagne, but of far broader sweep than simply the temporal power of the pope. The most radical danger inherent in the contamination of church authority by worldly power appears to reside in the use of anti-evangelical means for the service of the gospel, or what St. Hilary called "helping God by means of human usages." This danger is present because "human usages" are means that are not only "created," but also "subject to the sinfulness of creation." (See, in text 19, the parallelism drawn between "worldly ambition" and its subsequent incarnation in power, court dignities, imperial patronage, and so on.)

The basic element in this usage is that it comes to be *erected into a structural, theoretical principle* instead of being allowed to appear only in occasional or limited cases, which are exceptional by their very nature. This prevents these means, once assumed, from being criticized (2, 26). A theoretical, structural acceptance of such means entails two very serious consequences:

— God is falsified. Our texts speak of "idolatry," a "commerce in Christ" (15, 16), or "regarding the might of Christ as impotent" (19).

— The agent employing these means is contaminated or corrupted. Dante criticizes the greed of Nicholas III (15, 16), and St. Hilary the "ambition of power" (19).

And now an inevitable division appears among Christian people between those who enjoy the use of these means (theoretically to serve Christ, but in practice as "addicted" to them) and those who do not. In the literary language of Dante, the "keys" are then converted into a "battle flag," and the poet goes so far as to say—erroneously (see Matt. 23:1–3)—that in the eyes of Christ the throne of Boniface VIII is vacant (17).

### 1.2. Post-Tridentine Texts

This anthology has evidenced the disappearance of much internal criticism after the time of Luther and the French Revolution. This is not due simply to the success of the post-Tridentine reforms. It is in part owing to the unfair advantage taken by Luther of sincere criticisms like those of Adrian VI, with the resulting loss of enthusiasm on the Catholic part for continuing to make any such criticism. Finally, it is also owing to the fact that, beginning in the eighteenth century, the church felt itself to be more intensively under attack from without. True, it may be that the church might well have asked itself to what extent it had occasioned these attacks. But be this as it may, the fact remains that criticism from within began to be replaced by criticism from outside the church.

This specious interior serenity did not prove ultimately beneficial. Little by little the church began to close in upon itself— curl up and perhaps doze off. It remained for the twentieth century to feel the urgency that rings only in prophetic voices in the nineteenth. The church was in need of a profound change, a structural change.

As we have observed, modern criticism echoes certain themes of the past. Concretely, these themes are the two that emerge most clearly on our balance sheet: a preference for the poor, and the exercise of authority.

However, modern criticism inevitably finds its own accents.

As we have observed several times, more recent criticism tends to be directed against structural shortcomings rather than personal conduct. Perhaps the most frequent target of modern criticism is what would later come to be called "ecclesiocentrism" — an image of a church centered on, closed in upon, itself, thinking only of itself and obsessed with its own survival, so that even when it declares that it is proclaiming the Word, it actually seems more attentive to the splendor and the authority that accrue to it in virtue of that proclamation than to the comprehension and acceptance of the Word proclaimed. This ecclesiocentrism was described by I. F. Görres as a matter of "such zeal for the defense of the powerful ecclesiastical positions, and so little for the growth of the Reign of God" (33). Görres regards this shortcoming as springing from a fear of the future, and from the temptation of security at all costs — accompanied, of course, by an insistence that the security in question is for the sake of the mission. Text 32 criticizes a paradigmatic example of this temptation of security, which becomes blind to the *price* at which that security is purchased ("bayonets," "ruinous scandals," and so on²), forgetting that the gospel was not propagated thanks to a secure footing in this world, but thanks to the content of the proclamation. Rahner defined this temptation of security as a "fear of the future, a triumphalism of the past, and a suspicion of any present not created by [the church]." This is the temptation that provides the occasion for the heated diatribes of a Papini (34–37), all of them consistently reducible to a single intuition: the official church is composed no longer of missionaries, but of functionaries. It is not that these functionaries are corrupt. But they are installed and established; therefore they are mediocre.

It is the temptation to security that, it seems to me, epitomizes and subsumes the targets of all of the accusations we have seen in the modern texts. All the evils decried seem to spring from this single root. An overriding concern with security will spawn a mistrust of the laity, a preaching devoid of content or proclamation of the good news (33), a mistrust of science, the burden of bureaucratic inertia (41), and so on. It will likewise occasion deficiencies in relations with the other Christian churches: a lack of love and appreciation for separated Christians, a unilateral absolutization of our own truth (41). Finally, it will be deleterious to the relationship between the church and the world, which will now be based on common convenience rather than on the risk of love, and will therefore be unable to recognize its hours of destiny and turn them to account (41). Our texts give the inescapable impression that all of these phenomena derive and spring from that more radical affliction to which we refer as ecclesiocentrism.

### *1.3. Theological Elements*

Thus we have a very rapid synthesis of the content of both our pre-Tridentine and our post-Tridentine criticisms. But along with that content, our texts contain sufficient elements for us to be able to sketch a *theological* reflection on the very fact of criticism in the church. And to this I shall devote the final part of this rapid accounting.

The elements that I am about to assemble refer at times to the church itself, and at times to the voice of criticism in the church. These might all be synthesized, however summarily, in a single compound thesis: *The church does not cease to be holy by the fact of being criticized; on the contrary, its holiness places it under the obligation to listen to criticism. And the critic does not become holy by the fact of criticizing; on the contrary, in virtue of being of the church, the critic is obliged to offer the criticism in a holy manner.* Needless to say, I shall incorporate the texts of the second and third part of this anthology, as well, into the following reflection, as it is they that have provided the most useful material for our new purpose.

### A. The Holiness of the Church

1. Where the holiness of the church is concerned, several of our texts insist on that paradoxical, frequently observed duality of a church that is "of this world," hence corrupt, and at the same time the "Spouse" of a Christ who will not leave her in peace but will harass her until she returns to him. This is the mystery of "spirit in flesh," of which every human being on the face of the earth is the vehicle, but which the church incarnates and intensifies in a special way: as a "sign of salvation." We

might reformulate our text 14 to the effect that as every human being is *simul iustus et peccator*, so the church, in yet a sharper paradox, is the *casta meretrix*. This dual condition of the church attaches to it in virtue of its quality as "paradigm of humanity," hence paradigm of both grace and sin (48). Legitimate criticism is simply and solely an expression of this duality. To deny the legitimacy of all criticism through an appeal to the supernatural element in the church would be to fall into an error analogous to the docetist heresy. St. Augustine's observation that there will always be hierarchs who will make use of their dioceses for their own honor and convenience (52), or Durandus's comment that the pope has received no license to sin with the bestowal of the See of Peter (20), represent more than a psychological observation. They constitute a theological principle. God has not made the church impeccable. Such is not the holiness that God has bestowed upon it. Neither, for that matter, does God wish to dispense the church from the laws governing the operation of any large social body. If, as Pius XII asserts, the very nature of the body social calls for criticism, then to deny the legitimacy of that criticism will be to betray, once more, a docetist or monophysite conception of the church (57). It will represent a conceptualization of the church as a disembodied spirit. And denials of this type, as every psychologist knows, create the ideal conditions under which this "body," currently rejected, or even regarded as nonexistent, will be free to nibble away in secret at the Spirit dwelling within it. Inasmuch, then, as it is both a theological principle and an observation from experience, the phenomenon Augustine observes in our text 52 is simultaneously to be accepted and combated. The church, *this* church, is tò be accepted "as is"; but the concrete individuals who are "this way" are to be combated and corrected. Criticism, therefore, inasmuch as it can perform both tasks at once, has the potential to be a testimonial of unity (52)—but only of that mysterious unity of the holy and the sinful that we find in the church of God.

2. From this dualism of holiness and sinfulness, or of Spirit and "flesh," in the church (although the church is not necessarily identified with these elements), flows a second duality: that of charism and power. Any totalitarian society can proclaim that the vehicle of power is the vessel of the spirit of that society.

But, as Rahner insists, power and Spirit do not necessarily coincide in the church (59, 60). And Rahner draws a number of conclusions from this fact. He concludes to the possibility of error in the official church. He concludes to the possibility that valid truths or initiatives expressing the will of God may spring from below instead of from above. He concludes to a very broad concept of the "life of the church," which now must include more than obedience. But most important of all, he concludes that the duality in question is structural in the church, and willed by God; and that therefore the oneness, the unity, of the church is a *koinonia* of dialectical tension, not a suppression of that tension through the elimination of one of the two poles, the hierarchical or the charismatic. And all of this leads Rahner to maintain, in virtue of the very definition of infallibility, that the coercive and compelling powers of the church exist only for exceptional situations, and ought not to be employed in the ordinary activity of the official church. And what is reserved for exceptional cases cannot be the sole font of one's activity (59). To this we should add that the exceptional situation must be recognized to be at hand not only when unity is threatened, but when uniformity threatens to destroy pluralism.

But if this is the nature of the church's holiness, then far from invalidating all criticism and rendering it illegitimate, it is precisely the holiness of the church that requires criticism. The permissibility of criticism in the church springs primarily from the constitutive paradox of the church: the church is holy, and it is made up of sinful human beings. If the church is holy, then precisely it *must* demand more of itself, though it be made up of human beings (49). Not: since the church is holy, it is the more to be praised. And thus the fact of criticism ought to be the basis of the most radical distinction between the church and other institutions. With the latter we may be more tolerant. After all, this is "the way people are." There is something astonishing, then, in criticism of the church, something insane to the logic of the world, something that that logic would label "insolence" ("That the last should address the first, or the poor the powerful!" [42]) or "meddling" (as someone might ask St. Columban who appointed him judge over his fellow human being [42]). But the wisdom of the world is shattered (see the same text 42): first, in the gospel there is *neither first nor last*; and second, the church belongs to *each of its members*, and no one is exempt from the responsibility to "edify" it, construct it, improve it. Precisely because it is theirs, all will love it more than they love the positions they occupy in it. The pope will love the church more than his papacy, the faithful will love it more than their own tranquility. Both reasons lend St. Columban the courage to be forthright. However, he feels constrained to add a third consideration, one springing from human reason or common sense: when the church is under attack from without (from the side of the "Arians," the enemies of the church), criticism from within will obviously be invulnerable to the charge that it is insolence or meddling. It is easily seen as but loving concern (42) — albeit mingled with pain.

A number of texts argue along these same lines. Factors sometimes appealed to as reasons for *not* criticizing the church (the holiness, the dignity, and so on, of the church) are precisely the considerations that constitute the theological basis *for* such criticism. The sole proviso is that these factors be understood in their eschatological sense. The author of text 49 and the authors of a number of other pre-modern texts cited above did not know the modern expression "eschatological reserve," it is true; but they knew its meaning. The church appeals to the eschatological reserve against the actual development of history. Deprived of their eschatological note, the church's holiness, dignity, and so on could be distorted into sheer worldliness. Criticism can prevent this. That is why a St. Augustine, or a John of Paris, are so insistent that the very holiness of the church is the factor that places it under the obligation of listening to criticism (51, 45). And it is in virtue of the very holiness of the church that that church cannot be loved without requiring of it what belongs to it by reason of its holiness (33). God loves individual human persons — who possess nothing of their own but sin — by forgiving them (Rom. 5:8ff.). But to refuse to be demanding of the church would be tantamount to abandoning one's faith in its holiness. Of course, the demand must be the demand of a lover (43).

3. The urgency of that demand is sharpened still further by another consideration adduced in several of our texts. In virtue of the duality of the constitution of the church, its wicked mem-

bers conceal its good members (10, 25). The evil render the good invisible. This provides an excellent pretext for attacking the church and rejecting its authority. It occasions the "growth of anticlericalism" (25), paving the way not only for Luther but for later anticlericalism as well. But when, by the very fact that they make the criticism, critics take their distance from the phenomena of this breach, they thereby testify that they know the holiness of the church to be intact. They know that many others of its members continue to be holy, however hidden and however less "official" (10, 24), perhaps, in human eyes. After all, these holy members will be more "official" in the eyes of God. As John of St. Thomas put it, "heaven [the element of holiness in the church] is not the mere activity of the pope, but the holy activity of any of its members." That is, the church is represented (before God) not by its hierarchs, but by its saints.

Hence arises a series of serious demands to be made on the hierarchy, in their capacity as the "officialdom" of the church in human eyes. In the case of evangelical authority, the moral obligation attaching to authority as such is greater, is "multiplied" (61). To be authority in the church does not mean to *have* more holiness and consequently more love. To be authority in the church means to be much more *obliged* to love more. Thus the more a person is a person of the church, the more that person ought to welcome criticism, rather than being the more irritated by it or believing it to be the more iniquitous (63). Of course, this proposition must be complemented with its correlative: the more ecclesial one's criticism, the more it must be directed against oneself. And to both propositions must be added: not for purely human reasons, but for strictly theological ones. The church is "the world inside out" — though it not be such in the eyes of that world. And these demands culminate in a consideration put forward by some of our texts apropos of the church of Rome. Some of our passages read like a paraphrase of St. Ignatius of Antioch's typification of that church as one of "superabundant love." Durandus believes that Rome should be a "mirror" — not, however, proclaiming itself as such, but by acting as such (20). Adrian VI and the cardinals preparing for the Council of Trent saw it as the "head of holiness," but distinguished the content of this expression from the mere accumu-

lation of power, since power corrupts it (by occasioning adulation, by functioning as a "Trojan horse," etc.; see texts 27–29);
and then it is no longer the "head of holiness."

4. The last object of our ecclesiological reflection will be a
product not of the duality of holiness and sin, nor of charism
and power, nor of officialdom before God and officialdom in
human eyes—but a product of a duality known to the church
better than to anyone else: the duality of the church and God.
However necessary the mediation of the church, the church does
not absorb the totality of the individual's relationship with God.
Rahner formulates the reason for this in a manner altogether
typical of Ignatian spirituality. God, he explains, has a particular
will with regard to every human being, and in each concrete
situation. Universal laws supply this particular will with a certain
negative and approximative criterion. But they do not translate
it mechanically and adequately. And yet the "abdication of conscience" is a great temptation in the church, as well on the part
of the institution (for the sake of functioning more effectively,
by worldly standards) as on the part of the individual (for convenience, security, "buying heaven," and so on). In this context
Rahner coins the expression "collectivism of hearts." Rahner's
concept bears close attention. The church is very sensitive to
certain aspects of other collectivities. If it hopes to convey the
impression that its concern is legitimate, it had better maintain
that same sensitivity in its own regard (see text 58).

Rahner brings forward two reasons the church must avoid
this "collectivism of hearts." The first is profoundly theological.
God is not content with our "paying him back" for all that he
has done for us. God wants the depths of us. God wants the
firstfruits of the new humanity that is about to dawn in the life
of each of us (58). The other reason is a more contingent one.
In light of the twentieth century experience of totalitarianism,
the sin of scandal inherent in ecclesial repression of criticism
becomes grave indeed. The church may not permit itself to give
the impression that it believes in a sort of (may I be forgiven
the expression) "ecclesiastical Leninism," in virtue of which a
"church for itself"—composed of church leaders and the repo-
sitory of "genuine ecclesiality" and the "true church conscience"—would subsist side by side with a "church in itself"—

whose sole duty would be to follow the other. This conception is contrary not only to modern sensibility, but to the very gospel (cf. 57).

## B. Ecclesiality of Criticism

The second part of our ecclesiological reflection on criticism in the church will regard the author of the criticism. However, like our consideration of the holiness of the church, it will be a pneumatological reflection, a reflection on the Spirit—here, on the Spirit in the church. The Spirit who builds the community is not available to manipulation. It is free to breathe where it will. Thus true criticism in the church is not a privilege of dignity or holiness (44) or office (45). It is simply the fruit of a gospel that scorches your hands (46). The critic's attitude toward the object of criticism can be like that of a beast of burden toward a prophet (Balaam's ass), or of the "last" in the presence of the "first" (42, 25), of a voice crying in the wilderness (1), and so on. In the most desperate situations, critics may have more hope of avoiding harm to the people than of actually effecting any correction (1). In more serene reflections one may regard one's intervention as a work of mercy (44), or of the zeal of charity (45). Here, Augustine warns, the dialectic of truth and appropriateness must be perceived not as a dilemma between speaking and keeping silent (as there will always be someone for whom truth will be appropriate and silence not), but rather as a choice among manners of speaking (47). Even this consideration, however, which will impose certain conditions on criticism, will not automatically secure a successful outcome. The reason is not necessarily the wickedness of the objects of criticism. Rather (following Rahner's matchless realism here) it is the plurality of situations and human psychologies. This plurality is in itself conflictual, although all Christians are called upon to seek to render it harmonious, or in any case respectful (57). It will likewise be well to recall Rahner's subsequent observation that the training received in the church (by laity and clergy alike) is deficient. We must learn to catch the wind, seize the moments of the Spirit. We must acquire a connaturality with the spirit of criticism—as well as a sense of due measure with regard to criticism, lest we mistake the right to criticize for a license to criticize unrestrainedly. And we must learn to steep our criticism in love and loyalty. We are deficient in these things, and the reason is that *charism entails suffering* (59): charism bears with it a cost. Further, charism supposes an acceptance of the plurality of gifts, and thereby precludes any attempt to monopolize the Spirit, even when someone else is attempting to do so (59, 60). The image of Ezekiel as evoked by Origen (62), or that of a love willing to suffer for the beloved, far from lulling us to sleep (33, 64), are the best images of this suffering, which will always have to be borne if criticism is not to degenerate into condemnation. Criticism can make us an instrument of God. By condemnation we arrogate to ourselves the place of God. The difference must never disappear.

## 2. LOOKING AHEAD

Following this rapid, incomplete synthesis, which in no way claims to supplant what our texts themselves have to say, the question arises of itself: what would our authors say *here and now*? I ask this question not in the spirit with which a journalist might hope to back an interviewee into a corner and come up with a little sensationalism; I ask it in the spirit of believers who have an inquiry to make out of love for the church. And this question is the great question of many men and women of today, who clash with the church, or who at least address to it the evangelical question, "Are you the one who is to come, or do we look for another?" God forbid it ever cease to be asked because of having long since received an answer in the negative.

But it is a question church leaders are all too prone to dismiss. All too readily, the hierarchy regard it as surely arising out of some immature, adolescent utopianism, or as posed by someone with an "axe to grind," or simply as emerging from ill will.[3] A like attitude contains the reason *every great institution* (religious or lay) *can only be conservative*. Only ineffectual "ghetto" movements can permit themselves to be progressive. Large institutions, being nonpersons, are wholly governed by the institutional drive. And the institutional drive is constituted primarily of an instinct for self-preservation. Hence the mind-boggling fact that institutions can make progress only when fertilized by the sacrifice of persons—the persons we call prophets.

But once we recognize the reason that institutions find themselves in this position, we find it useful to apply to them the words of Cardinal Suhard: "Do some of them not fall into the very excess they reprehend? Is the defense or repulsion reflex to which they yield always more clear-sighted and charitable than the appetite for novelty that they stigmatize?"[4]

There is a dose of reason in the institutional reaction. But it is insufficient to invalidate Cardinal Suhard's question. In a secularized, plural world, of which the church is no more than a minoritarian part (called to be a sacrament of the salvation of Christ), the official conduct of that church is no longer a mere question of fidelity or infidelity to God, of which God alone is the judge. That conduct now becomes a matter of the credibility or incredibility of the church. The apostles' proclamation would never have been believed had their lives remained the same as before they had heard the good news themselves. The case is the same today with the proclamation made by the church. Chapter 4 of Deuteronomy stipulates as a sign of Israel's closeness to God that the Israelites' laws be more just than those of other peoples. The primitive church could surely claim to have met this stipulation. Here there was "no more man or woman, Jew or Greek, master or slave." But we cannot, in all honesty, fail to recognize that the church of today, in its most official echelons, cannot make that statement. It is in need of reform.

This is a hard saying. Of this I am well aware. Let me therefore dwell on it for a moment. Once more, let me repeat that in making this statement I am attacking not particular persons, but structural deficiencies. And I gladly concede that the usual manner of life of ecclesiastics today no longer deserves the kind of criticism presented in Part 1. Ecclesiastics will be human beings till the end of time, but even an overdue reform of the church has borne undeniable fruit in the area of the personal life of its leaders. Indeed, in the freedom of the gospel we have already acknowledged that a certain relaxation in the customs of ecclesiastics in the area of sexual morality has appeared, paradoxically, in those elements in the church which had issued the loudest call for "change" and "reform," and who therefore have only discredited, if not mortally wounded, their own cause.[5]

But with the same freedom with which I have made the above concessions, we must also recognize that the astonishing changes of our times, together with the paralysis accompanying the Counter-Reformation, have occasioned the appearance of new obligations and new challenges, in function of new calls being issued by the Spirit. The danger is that we may be lukewarm or indecisive. (Of course, even the most "progressive" of us must continue to be strong and meticulous in the observance of what has "always been established.") And we must recognize that tepidity and indecision in the face of new imperatives can occasion more scandal than shortcomings in the implementation of "traditional" ones (which of course may be valid), precisely because it more deeply wounds the ethical sensibilities of the men and women of our world.

We speak of new challenges. And yet these challenges can be formulated in terms of three ancient themes—genuinely traditional themes that have pervaded our texts and constituted the balance sheet of the criticism we have seen, just as they will come to epitomize future exigencies. We daresay, then, that the Spirit seems to demand the conversion of the whole church today (1) in the matter of poverty and injustice, (2) in the exercise of authority (so far, the two great problems of the contemporary world as well), and (3) in what we have called "ecclesiocentrism," or the fear of not living for oneself, which so easily arises out of the present position of the church as a minority in a world that no longer coincides with ecclesial frontiers, a world enormously plural, a world that is secular or paganized. These are the wrinkles and blemishes that the Lord seeks to efface from his Spouse today.

This is not the proper moment to embark on an in-depth study of these themes. I cannot, however, sidestep my obligation to make one observation concerning each of them, and thereby bring to a close the investigation that is part of the core of this book.

### 2.1.

We hear it said that the church is excessively centralized— almost "Soviet" in this respect, and that its much-vaunted subsidiarity is in a sad state of repair. And we must confess that the usually exclusive role of Rome in the appointment of bishops is surely an infringement of the rights of the local church and a departure from both the New Testament record and the usage of the primitive church. On the occasion of the Second Vatican Council, we heard the emphatic demand that the Roman Curia cease to be a bureaucratic arm of the "center" against the "periphery" and place itself at the service of the authority of the church world-wide (the episcopal college, with its head, the Bishop of Rome). Likewise, apropos of the so-called "doctrinal processes," the 1971 Synod of Bishops made recommendations that were very valid, but which seem already to have been forgotten!

But these are concrete, particular demands, and we cannot attempt anything like an exhaustive enumeration here. The basic problem is the conversion of the entire church to the message of the gospel where the matter of authority is concerned. That message can be summed up under two heads: (1) the desacralization of authority, and (2) its transposition to a modality of service (a transposition not only at the level of the "intentions" of those who command, but at that of their concrete praxis as well).

Authority is absolutely necessary. God has not dispensed the church from this necessity. Of course, as Peter himself recalled, it is easier to pasture a flock "by tyranny than by becoming models for the flock" (1 Pet. 5:3). But only the latter is the gospel way. Every member of the faithful has at one time or another experienced the exercise of authority after the fashion of a guilt-imposing superego, capable of causing deep pain, even severe trauma, in persons of good will. Again every member of the faithful has experienced the exercise of authority as a necessary service, demanding at times, but always respectful, and ultimately beneficial to the group as well as to the individual. How often experience teaches us the difference between the application of exceptional measures in extreme situations, and the conversion of the exceptional into the normal. A Christian may not accept the primacy of might over communion, the supremacy of force over dialogue in the light of God's Word. Power must not be the solitary constructive recourse of the church.

Accordingly, I think that the best way to develop this point, especially in view of the tone of this book, will be to use another extensive citation. After all, our primary concern is not with particular demands, but with an evangelical change of heart vis-à-vis authority.

Between Vatican I and Vatican II — and it is hard not to recognize it — Rome feared (the popes or their curia) that Gallicanism might rise again, and, unfortunately, it used the prestige it had acquired or regained in 1870 to extenuate the exercise and the reality of the episcopate. First, there was an endeavor to admit to this function only men who were little capable of exercising it in a responsible fashion; then there was the business of restraining their action, peremptorily directing it, and even (quite simply) binding it hand and foot. The Modernism crisis, which arose between the two councils, served as a pretext or justification for completing what had begun.

Vatican II, without destroying or minimizing the doctrinal work of Vatican I — quite on the contrary, confirming it — proclaimed its desirable complements. But during the course of this council, and even more in what followed, it became apparent to what extent misunderstanding of the real sense of Christian authority was inviscerated in the consciousness of its possessors. Even though the doctrinal texts had formally acknowledged that conflict between primacy and collegiality can arise only in an ecclesiology of power, not in one of service, the episcopate again, in tending to its regeneration, too often thought of itself in terms of ecclesiological power. Even after the council, under the false cover of a restoration of collegiality, there were attempts to resurrect Gallicanism. In the council itself, it was shown to what extent the restoration of the power of a number of bishops signified capacity to act with regard to their subordinates exactly as they had reproached the "curia" for doing in the past. Neglect of the presbyterate and the priests of second rank in the conciliar deliberations and, even worse (when one thinks of it), the almost exclusive concern to bully them (though with honeyed words) constituted scandal for anyone who, desirous of reform, was exasperated by the long-latent crisis in the Church.

The "contestation of priests," which closely followed the council, deplorable as it was, not only in certain aspects but basically, is the inevitable consequence of such a reaction in the episcopate, of such misunderstanding among those in authority, who were responsible for the problem. But this contestation, in turn, showed how the deformation of authority (in its conception of itself) spread to the point that even those who rebelled against it remained imbued with it, to a degree they did not even suspect. What else is signified by claims that a priest be able to do secular work, marry, and especially, get involved in politics, if not a persistent, cruder, more brutal involvement than ever of the priesthood of second rank in the confusions which since the Middle Ages have adulterated, or tended to adulterate, the consciousness the priesthood of the first rank forged of its own function. It was thought that an adult presbyterate had been attained because conciliar priests had overturned everything that had been painfully asserted since the seventeenth century in order to return (at least to priests of second rank) the Christian and spiritual sense of their vocation. They now claim for themselves, as their right, in this confusion between service and a function of the Church, a function that is secular, an autonomous affirmation of self, which for so long, and not only in appearance, had been the major temptation of the episcopate. . . .

Even among laity, at the moment the bishops thought they had associated them with their own emancipation, the same confusions obtain, and occupy, it seems, the whole terrain [Louis Bouyer, *The Church of God* (Chicago: Franciscan Herald Press, 1982), pp. 505-6].

## 2.2.

Sectors of humanity today have reached the zenith of refinement and luxury. And that same humanity is the stage of the most atrocious spectacles of malnutrition and misery imaginable.

The problem can no longer be dealt with solely at the existential level. Only a structural change of planetary proportions can remedy the situation. In this state of affairs, the demand of the gospel is more than clear. The church should be marching alongside those who do all that in them lies—to the point of laying down their lives—to bring more justice and solidarity to God's world. In fact, the church ought to be in the vanguard. Even where human beings culpably block the implementation of this demand for justice, the church should exhaust its voice and its strength in crying out, and demonstrating in deed, that God is on the side of those who are injured by this culpable default. And the church should do this even at the cost of "persecution for justice' sake."

Now, once more in all honesty, we Christians cannot fail to recognize that the concrete response of the church has lagged far behind what would seem to be the demand of the Spirit in this matter. The church was ever resplendent (in word and prophetic deed, as well as in its theological and spiritual foundations)[6] when charity was a personal, "private" virtue, and to be practiced in assistential fashion. However, today, now that love must be practiced *also* in structural and "macrocaritative" dimensions, the church gives the impression of withdrawing its prophetic voice and its theological foundations. Its actions in this respect give many generous, conscientious people the impression of tepidity, almost a lack of spontaneity, as if it performed those actions more as a sop to its own conscience than as an actual service to women and men. I, who am neither poor nor certain of fully loving the poor and really having embraced their cause, find it most uncomfortable to offer this criticism. But I dare to make it because the church itself, in the 1971 Synod of Bishops, has proclaimed:

> If the Christian message of love and justice fails to manifest its effectiveness in our activity for justice in the world, it will find it difficult to obtain credibility among the men of our time.... If ... the church is seen to be rich and powerful with the rich and powerful of this world, its credibility will be diminished [1971 Synod of Bishops; as cited in *Ecclesia* (1971), pp. 2297, 2299].

Now that the church itself has thus publicly acknowledged this challenge to its credibility—an acknowledgment renewed by Pope John Paul II in *Laborem Exercens*—what Christian will not have an obligation to come to its assistance when its credibility actually deteriorates on this point?[7] The "official" church today presents itself to the eyes of the world as much too much a house of the wealthy. Where the church as such is concerned, cruel as it may be to say so, Jesus' celebrated comparison is reversed and defeated: today it is easier for a camel to pass through the eye of a needle than for a poor person to enter the church and feel at home!

None of this is to deny that, in recent years, at the level of theoretical declarations, when it is a matter of words, a great deal has changed on this point, thanks in large part to the churches of the Third World and the steadfast, insistent voice of John Paul II. But what does not seem to change—and what therefore functions as partial cause of the anomaly just cited— is the *overall* praxis, or practices, of the church. Granted, even at the level of practice, marvellous, exciting things are happening in the churches of the Third World, and not only in Latin America. But it does not appear that, at the level of the wealthy churches and official echelons, such hopes meet with the welcome and the encouragement they surely receive in the heart of "the One who raised Jesus from the dead."

In my opinion, the reason for this lukewarm reception is fear rather than conscious fault. The church *fears* the poor, strange as it may seem to speak in this way. It fears them because they make it uncomfortable. It fears them because it has discerned that the change being asked of it would have a profound effect on itself. (After all, the church is first and foremost a church of the First World. Indeed, it may very well be that the astonishing development of that sector of the world, the fantastic dominion of the human being over the hard earth, is the fruit of its Christian matrix.) But it also fears them because it is afraid that, if it simply surrendered to them, it would be manipulated by them. It is this fear of being manipulated that is the clearest (and saddest) expression of the chasm that still yawns between the official church and the poor. Only if I have no very deep acquaintance with another can I fear manipulation by that other.

It is equally revealing that the church does not fear being manipulated by the wealthy (or at least not by the comfortable middle classes)—despite the fact that it is these groups, and not the poor, who are by far its most successful manipulators. But the cultures and interests of the church coincide with those of the rich, and this persuades the church that it has "no business out of its bailiwick." The feudalization of the church has been so pervasive that the church forgets, or unconsciously silences, certain points of its own classic moral doctrine—those points that would favor the poor of the earth and set the church in conflict with the powerful. (For example, we might recall the principle according to which "in extreme necessity, all things are common"; or the duty to pay a living family wage out of *commutative* justice, hence with the obligation of restitution; or we might consider the Latin American foreign debt, a sum of money so staggering that, on Catholic moral principles, these countries would scarcely seem bound in conscience to repay it.)

In this land of ours, where the machinery of history not only does not function today, but has never functioned—where the universal destiny of poor men, women, and children is suffering (although it may be a redemptive suffering)—we must no longer harbor illusions. For the day of reckoning is at hand. The Spirit is speaking to the churches of our land today. Let things be, then. Let matters take their course. Do not erect too many obstacles. Do not attempt to uproot the tares before their time, the time of harvest. Too often the obstacle is the near impossibility of merely living. Individuals and groups who will be light for the church of tomorrow where this problem is concerned are not allowed to live a life worthy of the name. It is a commonplace among us that the calvary of so many modern martyrs—who have come to be symbolized in the figure of their companion, Archbishop Oscar Arnulfo Romero—was not erected the day the murderers' bullet flew at their hearts. No, the gallows tree stood there long before.

### 2.3.

We have observed that the change being sought strikes fear into the heart of the official church. Perhaps this is because that church thinks it sees in such a change only a further loss of presence and power. After all, it lives in a world which it feels has already very much shoved it aside and deprived it of its influence. And this brings us to the last of the matters we have to consider.

All institutions have a tendency (and the more so, the more centralized the institution) to measure their internal well-being and external influence by the power and esteem of their central organism. Empires, for example, have often mistaken the prosperity of their center for the well-being of the whole empire. Such altogether elementary laws of societal functioning make it easier for us to understand why the loss of world leadership on the part of Rome, together with the practical liquidation of Christendom, should be felt in official church circles as a mortal attack on the church itself. Perhaps it ought not to seem strange that, despite so many declarations to the effect that the church exists not for itself but for human beings, so many persons charged with ecclesial responsibility, and doubtless of impeccable personal integrity, frequently give the impression that the church is entirely caught up in an obsession with its own survival. At all events the latter would seem to be the sole object of their labors. Doubtless the only intent of these ecclesiastics in the actions that convey this impression is to defend the church, to snatch the bark of Peter from shipwreck. But the suspicion that, deep within, these sincere individuals may harbor an unconscious need to defend their own quotas of power, or at any rate may cling to a fear little akin to faith, cannot be dismissed with a wave of the hand. Today more than ever, at a time when the church feels that it is "losing people," it should daily remind itself that "the Lord is its portion for an inheritance," and try not to lose sight of that logion of Jesus, valid for the church as for individuals, that "anyone who would save his life, loses it, while the one willing to lose it for the gospel, saves it."

After all, the gospel of Jesus, the goodness, the humane quality of the Christian God—these are not the sorts of things that materialize by way of some application of power, force, or sociological fraud. Power—regardless of the kind—can serve to avoid evils, perhaps many evils. But it is useless for manufacturing one whit of authentic good. Good is the freest thing there is, and can be served only by the unarmed strength of truth and the feeble might of love — two resources that, far from cancelling or manipulating human freedom, address themselves to it in order to enhance it. And although the church does not yet live in the fullness of love and truth, these constitute the goal toward which it should direct its steps, and it must not tolerate any administrative norms in its life other than those indispensable for apostles and teachers in the Spirit. Otherwise it will be leaving itself open to Louis Bouyer's harsh indictment: that of the "properly Catholic inertias."

> In limiting themselves to "conserving," "protecting," and "defending," the controlling agents of modern Catholicism were no longer able to guide, inspire, or elicit the living development of Catholic tradition in the whole body of the faithful. Therefore, despite themselves, they escaped a passive immobility, only to yield without resistance to external impulses. Under these conditions, they can no longer witness to the vitality of a body which still belongs to them, but in which too many of them, and for too long a time, no longer participate [Bouyer, *The Church of God*, p. 154].

If Bouyer is correct that it is the ecclesiocentrism of those who ought to be our teachers that deprives the faithful of guidance and inspiration for developing the Catholic tradition — then what a contrast between the peril of this inertia, and the horizons that open out when one thinks of getting beyond it! How beautifully this is expressed in the following words from the diary of that least ecclesiocentric pope of our century, John XXIII, penned only a few days before his death:

> Today more than ever, certainly more than in previous centuries, we are called to serve man as such, and not merely Catholics; to defend above all and everywhere the rights of the human person, and not merely those of the Catholic Church. Today's world, the needs made plain in the last fifty years, and a deeper understanding of doctrine have brought us to a new situation, as I said in my opening

speech to the Council. It is not that the Gospel has changed: it is that we have begun to understand it better. Those who have lived as long as I have were faced with new tasks in the social order at the start of the century; those who, like me, were twenty years in the East and eight in France, were enabled to compare different cultures and traditions, and know that the moment has come to discern the signs of the times, to seize the opportunity and to look far ahead [cited in Peter Hebblethwaite, *Pope John XXIII: Shepherd of the Modern World* (Garden City, N.Y.: Doubleday and Company, 1985), pp. 498–99].

## CONCLUSION

None of the criticism in this book is valid in virtue of the sheer fact of having been enunciated. No one knows this better than I, convinced though I am of the truth of the criticism I have transcribed. But at very least, the extracts here contained verify the statement of the church hierarchy with which I propose to bring this book to a conclusion. As we shall see, this statement is in perfect concord with the words of Pius XII that appear at the beginning of the book.

The church acknowledges the right of all to a proper freedom of expression and thought, which in turn supposes the right of every person to be heard in a spirit of dialogue calculated to maintain a legitimate variety in the church [1971 Synod of Bishops; as cited in *Ecclesia* (1971), p. 2299].

# NOTES

## PART 1

1. John Paul II was in Spain from October 30 to November 9, 1982. See *Origins* 12 (1982–83) for texts of key addresses given during that visit.

2. An ironical, untranslatable pun on the Pope's name. St. Bernard is comparing the name Eugene, "well born," to the flattering, toadying "Euge!" ("Well done! Hurrah!") of Psalm 40:15. St. Bernard's text reads: "... Qui dicunt tibi, Euge, Euge!" Thus he is implicitly citing Ps. 40:15: "let those who cry 'Well done! Hurrah!' at my downfall be horrified at their reward of shame" ["... qui mihi dicunt, 'Euge!'..."].

3. Another pun. Where we have translated "doings" and "dyings," St. Bernard has, respectively, *mos* ("custom") and *mors* ("death").

4. "Circumdatus varietate." Ps. 45:10 (Vulgate) described a young royal bride as "circumdata varietate" — "adorned in finery." (Modern scholarship prefers something more like the *New American Bible*'s "in gold of Ophir.")

5. All of the above passage from St. Bernard was translated from *PL* except the last two paragraphs, which do not appear in *PL* and were thus translated from the Spanish.

6. We have another example of this freedom of criticism in the celebrated, anonymous *Epistula Luciferi* ("Letter of Lucifer") addressed to Avignon Pope Clement VI, whose text, together with a bit of supplementary information, we here transcribe from the BAC *Historia de la Iglesia Católica*, 3:115:

"Lucifer, Prince of Darkness, Governor of the Mournful Empires of Deepest Acheron, Duke of Erebus, King of Hell, and Rector of Gehenna, to his Vicar the Pope and his Servants the Cardinals and other Prelates, those greedy Bishops who sprawl amidst delectation and carousing: health and benediction!

"We laud you, O Our beloved Babylon, for your eager toil in Our behalf, as for the assistance you render Us that We may emerge victorious over Our Enemy, the Christ, who seeks to exalt the poor and lowly against the Republic of This World. We commend you to Our beloved daughters, Avarice, Lust, and Pride, who, thanks to the Pope and his Cardinals, are all in excellent health. Should anyone preach or teach against you, crush him by your power of excommunication. We desire that you come to possess the positions We have prepared for you.

"Given at the Center of the Earth, in Our Palace of Darkness, etc. . . . "

"The letter was right on target," says Matteo Villani, "where the vices of our ecclesiastical shepherds were concerned. Many believed it to be the work of the Archbishop of Milan. . . . Actually its author was a Cistercian scholar called Petrus de Ceffonia, the author of many other writings worthy of study."

In view of its disputed origin, I have not included the "letter" in the text of this anthology. But it does serve as an example of the freedom of which Daniel-Rops has spoken. Further: it constitutes interesting evidence of the temptation of the hierarchy to respond to criticism with an abuse of the resources of ecclesiastical authority ("... crush him by your power of excommunication"). As we have seen, the sanction of excommunication came to be so casually applied that it eventually all but lost its force and could no longer be felt as a very serious penalty.

7. Henri Daniel-Rops, *Iglesia de la Catedral y de la Cruzada*, pp. 153–54, 121; the English translation of Daniel-Rops's book is *Cathedral and Crusade* (New York: E. P. Dutton, 1957), see pp. 120–21.

8. Cited in J. LeClerq, *Santa Catalina de Siena*, pp. 90–93; Fr. orig.: *Sainte Catherine de Sienne* (Tournai: Casterman, 1947).

9. H. Riedlinger, "Die Makellosigkeit der Kirche in den lateinischen Kommentaren des Mittelalters," *BGPTMA* 28/3 (Münster, 1958), pp. 244, 246–47, 249–50.

10. For the allegorical application of both figures, Rahab and Tamar, see Hans Urs von Balthasar, *Ensayos teológicos*, 2:261–76, 325–31.

11. "Ut Ecclesiam nanciscatur, ecclesiam deserit." I follow the Migne original in distinguishing between "church" and "Church" by lower case and capital letters, respectively. The distinction seems to be between the Church universal and a particular church.

12. The name of Dante will inevitably recall that of Petrarch (1304–47). The latter's verses, as finely hewn as Italy's marvellous columns and walls, are shattering:

> Wellspring of sorrow, hospice of wrath,
>  School of error, heresy's temple,
>  Rome! Babylon faithless and wicked,
>  Deaf to the sighs of thy countless mourners! [Canz. 138].

But with Petrarch it is even more difficult to distinguish his criticism of the church from his political activism (a confusion fostered, to be sure, by the twin sovereignty of the papal sway). For this reason, as well as for those to be cited below a propos of Erasmus and other more literary authors, I have decided to omit any Petrarchian texts from this anthology proper. The reader will find one more citation in *Historia de la Iglesia Católica* (BAC), 2:134.

13. Congar states expressly: "Durandus is no Gallican. But he does wish that papal power would be respectful of the authority of the bishops" (Yves M.-J. Congar, *Eclesiología desde San Agustín hasta nuestros días* [Madrid, 1976], p. 189).

14. From the 1671 Clousier edition.

15. The descriptions of Roman life presented in the *Relazzione* of Bernardo Navaggero, the Venetian Ambassador in Rome from 1558 to 1560, are really too hair-raising to quote, and are easily enough left to the reader's imagination.

But it may be of interest to cite the comment its reading drew from Francesc Cambó, one of the "fathers of Catalan."

"More shocking than the traffic in indulgences, worse than the scandals of the outwardly brilliant, showy pontificates of Alexander VI and Leo X, is that period of Roman decadence described by Bernardo Navaggero, which so encouraged the spread of Protestantism. General moral laxity, a corruption bereft of the least brilliance or glory, had the effect of driving the saints from Rome by natural repulsion, and of turning the stomach of a Henry VIII, who refused to consent that a power that could not maintain its own dignity would seek to impose it on him.

"The genuine miracle is that the Catholic Church, and especially, the human pontifical authority, could survive this period, presented by Bernardo Navaggero in such vile colors in his *Relazzione*" (Francesc Cambó, *Meditacions*, 2:332).

16. The verdict to the effect that the Tridentine reform came too late is based primarily on various passages from Luther, who wrote in 1528: "Long has there been a cry for a council, that the Church might be reformed by it" (WA 26:530). And in 1539 he commented: "The pope has refused to celebrate a council. He has no wish to reform the Church. Thus we have no other remedy than to seek a reform under the auspices of our Lord Jesus Christ" (ibid., 50:512). Luther rejected the token retouching that had been done by then as "matters of vestments and sandals" (ibid., 44:171). See Möhler: "In the first part of the fifteenth century, certain reformers within the Church attempted to get the needed changes under way, but their efforts were ridiculed

and scoffed at. Thereafter these reformers devoted themselves to reforming the Church from without" (*L'unité dans l'Eglise*, p. 231).

17. *Fontes Narrativi*, 3:677; 1:719.

18. As cited by Luis de Diego, *La opción sacerdotal de Ignacio de Loyola y sus compañeros* (Caracas, 1975), pp. 61–62.

19. On the other hand, the reader may have noted the absence of texts of perhaps the most popular of all of the critics of the church, St. Anthony of Padua (1195–1231), canonized in the very year of his death, and declared Doctor of the Church by Pius XII. I have no reason for this omission other than a lack of time and resources. A selection of such texts will be found in José María Díez Alegría, *Teología frente a sociedad histórica* (Barcelona, 1972), pp. 171–79, all of them from sermons by the saint, which is the most striking thing about them for purposes of our own study, as we shall observe in the following reflection. Likewise worthy of remark, however, is the grace and roguish humor with which St. Anthony addresses the targets of his criticism: "The Lord bade you feed, not fleece, his sheep. Joseph was sold by his brothers, and Jesus Christ is sold by the archbishops and other prelates. The bishops are as Balaam seated on his donkey [the church]: the donkey saw the angel of God, Balaam saw not a thing." Or we have St. Anthony's repeated comparison of bishops to brides or elegant ladies, riding out among the populace in elegance and finery.

20. Both texts are from Henri Daniel-Rops, *La Iglesia de los tiempos clásicos*, 1:32, 78.

21. Cited by Daniel-Rops, *La Iglesia de las revoluciones*, 1:426.

22. To all that has been said in the text must be added the fact that many of these criticisms originated with persons of impeccable, exemplary lives—individuals who embodied many of the ethical values of rationality, humanity, and so on, to which the champions of the Enlightenment were so attached. I might cite the storyteller of my own childhood, Tomás de Iriarte, whose stories and cautionary tales nurtured the ethical sense of so many bourgeois generations. What we did not know in those tender years is that Iriarte has a less well known fable than the one about the greyhounds and the curs or the monkey in the silk suit. It is called "Simon's Bark," and it speaks for itself. [I render the verse in prose—Tr.]

"Simon had a bark. Just a little fishing bark. But it was a fine bark. And he left it to his children.

"His children fished and fished. They became very wealthy. And Simon's bark became too small for them!

"So they improved it. They made it into a xebec. Then they made it into a frigate.

"Then into a warship. How its cannon roared!

"But this got them into a lot of trouble. And it wrecked their bark. Now Simon's bark is just an old hulk rotting in port. And it only seems like yesterday that it was such a fine little fishing bark! Ah, how time flies.

"A thousand times they've cleaned and caulked it. But it's still just a pile of trash.

"Do you know what they ought to do? Break it up. Throw most of it away. Somewhere within is still . . . Simon's bark! It was a fine bark!"

This fable cost Iriarte problems with the Inquisition, although he was ultimately not cited before the tribunal. In his *Historia de los heterodoxos españoles* (book 6, chap. 3), Menéndez Pelayo characterizes it as the "oldest heterodox poem I know in Spanish."

23. A fictitious character personifying the mediocrity of the German petit bourgeois — something like "Senyor Esteve" in Catalan literature.

## PART 4

1. The New Testament meaning of "worldly" is an ascetical meaning, referring not to the world as God's creation but as the locus of sin. See the biblical passage cited by Henry of Langenstein at the end of text 21.

2. And other costs that the text does not cite, such as the veto that could be exercised by certain political powers in a papal conclave. That "privilege" had the effect of elevating to the Sovereign Pontificate one Giuseppe Sarto — Austria having excluded Cardinal Rampolla — who as St. Pius X had the courage to abolish it at last.

3. Not all of them. An official text that appears to take this question very seriously was the Basque bishops' 1983 Lenten Pastoral, where we find following paragraphs:

"The world of work, thought, education, and health is withdrawing from the Christian community en masse. Some of these groups have moved from a combatitive attitude to one of indifference, reflecting an even more complete withdrawal. To be sure, there are many Christians among them. But all too frequently, these persons lack a fearless 'confessing faith.' . . . Perhaps they are persuaded that, while the 'product' they have to offer — the Gospel — is a quality one, the 'firm' that produces it — the Church — is not very reputable in these circles" (no. 9).

"All of the groups that we are about to describe have one thing in common: a negative image of the Church. Their members know of many Christians who are good persons and even good believers. But the Church universal, along with the local churches, to their way of thinking constitute a decadent institution, in an advanced state of decomposition, resistant to social change, attached to whatever elements of power it may still enjoy, estranged from the poor, inflexible in its dogmatism, evincing precious little tolerance for democracy ... and altogether too accommodating to the powers of this world" (no. 13).

And while it insists that "our churches do not merit such a negative judgment," the document nevertheless concedes that "if these men and women are to be able to accept Jesus as their Lord and the Gospel as the norm of their lives, what will be required is a Church renewed in its very sources, and thereby endowed with credibility" (ibid.).

Or again, concerning youth: "It is true that they perceive the Church as an 'unclean sign.' Then will we not make every effort not to defraud them, by striving to improve the Church?" (no. 16).

Finally, I should like to point out that this document also sets forth the three points emphasized in our "balance sheet": a church of the poor (no. 22), authority as service (no. 46), and ecclesiocentrism (no. 24).

4. *Documentation Catholique* (October 1945), cols. 1215–16.

5. I cannot examine the possible psycho-sociological explanations of this phenomenon in other shortcomings of the church to which it was a reaction.

6. The statement in parentheses is not a rhetorical one. The present anthology will be followed, God willing, by another, on the poor in Christian theology and spirituality.

7. *Laborem Exercens*, no. 8: The church regards the cause of the poor "as its mission and service. Its attachment to this cause must function as its verification of its fidelity to Christ."

# INDEX OF NAMES

*Bold face indicates pages on which a text is given in the anthology.*